Foundations of Education

Foundations of Education

A Social, Political, and Philosophical Approach

Jason C. Robinson

Canadian Scholars' Press
Toronto

Foundations of Education: A Sociological, Political, and Philosophical Approach
by Jason C. Robinson

First published in 2015 by
Canadian Scholars' Press Inc.
425 Adelaide Street West, Suite 200
Toronto, Ontario
M5V 3C1

www.cspi.org

Canadian Scholars' Press Inc. gratefully acknowledges financial support for our publishing activities from the Government of Canada through the Canada Book Fund (CBF).

Library and Archives Canada Cataloguing in Publication

Robinson, Jason, 1976-, author   Foundations of education : a social, political, and philosophical
approach / Jason C. Robinson.

Includes bibliographical references.
Issued in print and electronic formats.
ISBN 978-1-55130-720-6 (pbk.).—ISBN 978-1-55130-721-3 (pdf).—ISBN 978-1-55130-722-0 (epub)

   1. Education--Philosophy. I. Title.

LB14.7.R68 2015   370.1   C2014-907230-9   C2014-907231-7

Text design by Brad Horning
Cover design by Em Dash Design

Printed and bound in Canada by Webcom

Canad^{**}ä

MIX
Paper from
responsible sources
FSC   FSC® C004071
www.fsc.org

Contents

Acknowledgements

I owe a great debt to all of my teachers, to those within the classroom and those outside of its formality. I am most thankful for the gifts of time and care that encouraged a naive boy to learn something new, and thereby to see anew. Looking back I realize that I was not always the easiest student to work with, and yet there was always someone willing to offer patience and understanding. It was only a short time ago that I needed to learn how to learn—to discover the power of genuine questions and the freedom of being able to reason toward understanding. Education, whether in a narrow or broad sense, has rarely been an easy experience for me. There were more than a few embarrassing missteps and hurdles along the way. For some of us it takes longer to open up to the new and unexpected. We sometimes lack the kind of bold curiosity needed to venture away from the familiar. Indeed, some of us fight to remain in the dark, the comfortable place to which we have become accustomed. To all of my teachers and mentors, thank you for the push.

Setting the Foundations for a Philosophy of Education

This is a big-questions book meant to introduce the ongoing philosophical issues and problems related to education. The focus of this book is on five of the most influential philosophers of all time: Plato, Aristotle, Locke, Rousseau, and Dewey. All of these figures have had a lasting and significant impact on the philosophy of education—attention will be given to various conceptions of the nature, scope, and social and political relevance of education. No doubt there is a great deal left unsaid about the philosophy of education given our selective attention. However, these five individuals are undisputed champions in this area of philosophy, so we may be confident that many, indeed most, of the big questions in the philosophy of education are addressed in one respect or another.

This work offers four unique avenues of engagement. First, it is written in a manner that invites dialogue and reflection. Philosophy is about the creation of new and challenging conversations. By posing questions, it is hoped that you will take a moment to pause and reflect, critically evaluate, and judge the ideas presented, ideally forming a new dialogue with the concept. Moreover, while the suggested thought exercises may seem time consuming, it has been my experience that such exercises have surprising results. Sometimes it is not until we begin to question and develop our own ideas and philosophies that we begin to see how rich and nuanced the ideas of others are.

The second unique feature of this book is its tone. Many books on this subject contain a great deal of terminology that new readers of philosophy find difficult. The style and tone of this book, by contrast, should be accessible to most readers. When we do use unfamiliar vocabulary it will be explained clearly in the text or found in the glossary of terms.

The third unique feature of this book is that it examines the philosophy of education by focusing on the ideas of individual philosophers in respect to their broader perspectives. Only when a sense of the overall philosophy of each thinker is gained might we begin to appreciate their respective views on education. Too often a philosopher's ideas are presented in abstraction from the context of his or her philosophical perspective.

Finally, the fourth unique feature of this book is its historical breadth. We begin our investigation with ideas from Ancient Greece and finish with ideas born in 20th-century America—with about 2,500 years and a great deal of geography separating our first and last thinkers. There will be some striking similarities among our philosophers but also very strong contrasts. Indeed, this is part of what makes philosophy in general so controversial and exciting.

Though understanding education would be a simpler goal if we restricted our investigation to educational policies and institutions of formal learning, as philosophers, we must look at how education engages with being human. Developing a personal philosophy of education should not be confined to what happens in schools and formal settings.

WHAT DOES IT MEAN TO EDUCATE?

A great deal of debate has taken place around defining education. Some argue that unless we can define it we cannot hope to succeed at it. Others believe that we can only generalize about education, as there are simply too many forms and ideas encompassed by it. Is education a vast topic that cannot be defined completely? Perhaps, but there is still a great deal that may be said about education and learning:

- Education typically involves gaining or sharing knowledge of some kind (e.g., facts, data, or information). Whatever education is, it seems to involve the act of coming to know or the act of helping others come to know.
- Education often involves more than one person. The teacher-student paradigm often comes to mind when we try to define education.
- Education is usually associated with the young being taught by elders. This dynamic, representing a top-down model of those sharing life experiences and lessons with the less experienced, exists both within schools and at home.
- There are two important features of education: wisdom and practical know-how. A good education will help us apply knowledge outside of the classroom or home.

Basically, education is an experience in which people learn knowledge, practical skills, and wisdom. But is it only human beings that possess the power to learn? What about plants and animals? Consider the banana plant in my home. The interesting thing about this plant is that when placed on the left side of the window it starts to grow toward the right, toward the light. When switched to the other side of the window the plant adjusts again. Does this indicate a kind of learning in the form of adaptability? Does this plant *know*? Consider my cat: when he wants food, he meows until we feed him. If he wants to go outside, he might meow and paw at the door to get our attention. He did not know how to do these things as a kitten. It would be very strange if we sent our pets to college or university. However, it is not at all strange to send a dog to obedience school. But why do we say that we train animals but educate people? We may train people, too, but this term does not usually possess the same fullness as the term educate. Most of us would probably agree that the major distinctions between training and education, especially when talking about dogs and humans, have to do with the degree and type of learning involved. This leads us to another question that is very important to our investigation. What is unique about human education?

TWO UNIQUE FEATURES OF HUMAN EDUCATION

Time: One of the biggest differences between human beings and animals and plants is the incredibly long period of time we devote to education. It is not enough to simply know how to read, write, and do basic math. Perhaps an example of this trend is the growing number of people with bachelor's, master's, and doctoral degrees. It was once fairly rare to have a general bachelor's degree, but today it is becoming almost commonplace. By the time someone graduates with a BA, he or she will have spent between 15 to 18 years in school. To get a competitive edge today, many students will add a master's degree to the list, which means another two or three years.

Breadth: Education reflects our unique ability to think about the distant future. We are able to be systematic and creative in our planning for a reality that does not yet exist. Moreover, we think historically, often ruminating on our personal histories as well as much broader cultural histories. One indicator of intelligence is the ability to anticipate and prepare for the future based on one's understanding of the past. A philosophy of education must take into account much more than the needs and demands of the present.

WHAT IS PHILOSOPHY?

The term **philosophy** comes from two words: *philos* and *sophy*. *Philos* is from the Greek for *love* or *lover*. *Sophia* is the Greek for *wisdom*. To be a philosopher is to be a lover of wisdom, to be in pursuit of wisdom. Many of us are accustomed to making a distinction between knowledge and wisdom. Knowledge, generally speaking, has to do with facts or information that may be written down for others to read. Wisdom, by contrast, includes knowledge but goes much deeper. If one is wise one is able to apply knowledge. Additionally, real wisdom is something that comes through experience; it is not merely something that we gain by reading about it, although that may certainly help. Philosophy is about more than knowledge, for it includes all human experience as its subject matter.

It has been argued by many that to be human is to be a philosopher—we cannot avoid philosophical questions. We may, however, think philosophically with varying degrees of sincerity and success. The underlying assumption here is that the more thorough and sincere our efforts, the more clarity and insight we will gain, the closer to wisdom we will be.

There are four main (overlapping and converging) ways of describing the activities of philosophy: **Speculative**, **Analytic**, **Existential**, and **Phenomenological**.

FOUR CLASSIC APPROACHES TO PHILOSOPHY

Speculative: The speculative approach to philosophy is characterized by a big picture mentality. Speculative philosophy represents the most popular image of traditional philosophy. Though not necessarily the most popular version of philosophy today, especially among North American philosophers, the speculative version has a long history in Western thought. Speculative philosophers try to answer big questions about human reality and experience as a whole in order to offer a comprehensive view of meaning, reality, and existence. Speculative philosophy has most recently come under severe attack from analytic philosophers in the Anglo-American tradition. In the most radical sense of the criticism, speculative philosophy is said to be an impossible and meaningless venture. No one is capable, they argue, of answering the sorts of questions raised by speculative philosophers. Instead, we ought to focus our attention on more possible goals, specifically a systematic analysis of our concepts and language.

Analytic: The analytic approach to philosophy is characterized primarily by its emphasis on the analysis of language as the main and proper aim of every philosopher. As a much more recent development within the larger tradition of philosophy, analytic philosophers see within the (speculative) tradition of philosophy many mistakes, confusions, and seemingly unsolvable puzzles. These, they argue, are rooted in misunderstandings of language. In most analytic philosophy textbooks today you will find an emphasis on critical analysis, clarity in terminology and concepts, and precise argumentation as the primary criteria for philosophical meaning. One of the popular criticisms of analytic philosophy is that it relies, either directly or indirectly, on the verification principle. This principle argues that a statement, any statement, is meaningful if and only if it is true by virtue of definition or if it is verifiable by observation—in other words, via one of our five senses. If a statement is not subject to either form of verification it is meaningless. That is not to say it is untrue or false. It is simply meaningless if it cannot be verified in one of these ways. Thus theological and metaphysical statements cannot be the proper subject of philosophical thinking. You cannot really define or observe God. This principle is widely regarded as inadequate today, even among analytic philosophers, yet the basic assumptions behind it remain very influential, namely a preoccupation with clarifying statements (propositions). Many have argued that this way of thinking is a case of missing the forest for the trees. Not only is the principle an unreliable test of meaning (or meaninglessness), but this way of looking at meaning risks ignoring much larger concerns and questions in philosophy.

Existential: The existential approach is characterized by its disdain for abstractions, rules of logic and argumentation, and obsession with objectivity. A proper philosophical analysis must focus on the human being in its practical encounters with others and the world. Existentialists often perceive contemporary humanity as suffering a crisis of authenticity and meaning. We have, according to many existentialists, allowed ourselves to be lost to technological and philosophical trivialities, and we have forgotten ourselves, our true authentic selves. A common criticism of both the existential and phenomenological (below) methods of philosophy is that they are too subjective to offer significant standards and criteria for judging what is true or false, meaningful or meaningless, and so on. At bottom the criticism seems to be that while these two approaches, as well as the speculative, may ask very interesting questions that involve important aspects of our lives, they fail to be robust or rigorous enough to stand up to serious reflection and analysis.

Phenomenological: The phenomenological approach is characterized by a focus on what is given or what appears in our consciousness of things. Phenomenology is interested in what is seen or directly experienced. If we are to understand our experiences we must do more than what the analytic philosophers are interested in doing. A phenomenological account of human understanding begins, like the existential view, with the concrete experience each of us has in our ordinary encounters with the world. There are different kinds of practices within phenomenology. Edmund Husserl and Martin Heidegger, for instance, are both phenomenological thinkers, but they differ significantly on how we ought to analyze human understanding.

Some of us tend to think more logically, technically, and precisely about philosophical issues, looking for objective and absolute answers, while others like to think about more broad, aesthetic, and subjective questions. These two ways of thinking are not mutually exclusive, but philosophers conventionally emphasize one over another.

As we proceed through the chapters, try to keep the following four views about philosophy in mind. It will help to routinely ask yourself how you think the various problems of education might be approached and answered through each philosophical lens.

Divisions of Philosophy

There are four major categories of philosophers. These labels, which are by no means exhaustive or definitive, represent the different kinds of questions posed and the methods used to pursue answers. Discussions in the philosophy of education may take place through the lens of any of the following philosophical approaches: **Metaphysics**, **Epistemology**, **Logic**, and **Value Theory—Ethics** and **Aesthetics**. These major divisions or branches of philosophy are at the core of philosophical thought and allow us to frame most questions meaningfully. Developing a philosophy of education involves carefully crafting paths across all four divisions of philosophy.

FOUR MAJOR CATEGORIES OF PHILOSOPHY

Metaphysics: The term *metaphysics* comes from the Greek, *meta*, meaning after or beyond, and *physis*, meaning nature. Metaphysics is the study of that which is beyond nature or physical reality. Originally the term came from *meta ta physika*, literally the books that came after the books about physics in Aristotle's corpus of writings. Metaphysics is the study of reality, but unlike physics, metaphysics is the branch of philosophy that deals with principles of being (**ontology**) and the structure of existence. Often abstract, it has two extremes. The first extreme focuses on reality that exists outside the natural realm, a world beyond our abilities to touch, taste, see, and smell. The second extreme focuses only on the material realm, for it is believed that there is nothing more than the material. In a typical book on metaphysics you would see the following kinds of chapter headings: "The Mind as a Function of the Body," "Freedom and Determination," "Fate, Space and Time," "Time and Eternity," "Causation," "God," "Being and Nothingness," and so on.

Part of being educated means being better able to deal with or work in the world. It needs to be asked, "What do we mean by 'the world'?" From a metaphysical perspective (as opposed to something like a physical perspective, i.e., scientific) this question is asking about fundamental reality. Is reality only the physical or is there more to be said—something about what is above, beyond, behind the physical? We will soon discover why it is that metaphysical questions are very important for some philosophers, such as Plato. While we may look at the world and see something that appears to be more or less stable and predictable, some metaphysicians look at the world and see something behind it that is even more stable and sure. This makes the truth of our perceived world less reliable than the unseen world, a greater reality than this reality. In our culture, there is a widespread assumption that the universe is governed by knowable laws—in other words, laws of nature. These assumptions radically shape how we define good education. Are there laws of nature? Is there a role for randomness, chance, and chaos? Are there accidents that happen even though they might violate our understanding of the laws of nature? How you answer metaphysical questions will very much influence your philosophy of education.

Epistemology: The term *epistemology* comes from the Greek, *episteme* (knowledge). It is the branch of thought that deals with principles of knowledge and human knowing. Philosophers often refer to two types of knowledge: *a priori* knowledge, or reason alone, and *a posteriori* knowledge, in which rational justification requires reference to experience of some kind. We will be hearing about both forms of knowledge shortly. A large part of the problem of knowledge concerns the relationship between truth and belief or opinion. While we may have true or correct belief about something, this is different from true knowledge, which must have further justification beyond mere opinion and belief. When doing epistemology one asks many questions, such as: What is knowledge? What does it mean to know? How is knowledge acquired? May we really know anything for certain? When I say I know something, what do I mean? How may I attain justified true belief?

One of the biggest epistemological questions concerns the source of knowledge as something from our senses. May we trust our senses? The classic example of the problem of sensed knowledge (or empirical knowledge) is a simple one. Consider a pencil in water, both held in a glass. If you look through the glass the pencil will appear broken or warped, and yet if you remove the pencil from the water it is intact. Which is true? Based on our sensed knowledge alone, we would believe the pencil to be broken when it is not.

Epistemological questions are important to all of us. As a species, we engage in a lot of activities, whether those be for our careers, families, hobbies, or otherwise. Some of us are able to build houses, compose symphonies, develop vaccines, and innumerable other things. Humans have a great range of capabilities, and yet one of the things that tie all of our activities together is our ability to think or know. Our educational theories must be based on sound epistemological considerations. You may sometimes hear people talk of education in terms of content and skills. Some prefer to emphasize content—for example, information, facts, data—while others prefer to emphasize skills, such as practical know-how or ability to critically analyze. Whether you are learning content or skills (or both at the same time), you will be relying on your ability to know.

Logic: The term *logic* comes from the Greek, *logos*, for *word, argument, account, reason*, and *study*. Logic is the branch of philosophy that deals with principles of reasoning and is used as a tool to clarify thought. A course in logic may be either formal or informal. In a formal logic course, you are likely to learn about very specific ways of mapping or conceptualizing language. This will involve signs and symbols necessary to help formalize thinking and language patterns. In an informal logic class you are likely to learn about common mistakes of reasoning called fallacies. Informal logic classes spend a lot of time examining how popular forms of reasoning, such as common sense, often go wrong. Such a course may also deal with problems in scientific reasoning.

Value Theory: Ethics and aesthetics fall under the larger field of philosophy known generally as value theory. Value theory covers a range of approaches to understanding how, why, and to what degree people value things—whether the thing valued is a person, idea, or object.

1. Aesthetics: From the Greek *aesthesis*, meaning perception by the senses, aesthetics focuses on the value pertaining to art and beauty. When thinking about aesthetics, we would investigate matters such as the nature of beauty, how truth is connected with beauty, and whether beauty, art, and knowledge are related.
2. Ethics: From the Greek, *ethos*, meaning *character, disposition, custom, habit*; it is the study of moral, social, and political values. Ethics is the branch of philosophy that deals with questions concerning the rightness or wrongness of actions. Ethics may be both highly theoretical, such as thinking about what is of ultimate worth and the best kind of life for all humankind, and it may be also very practical, such as questioning justification for specific decisions about right and wrong, prescribing action and choices. By and large value theory asks us to consider the meaning of life, if any. Your conception of meaning will impact not only if but also how you believe it ought to be taught.

Human Nature and the Philosophy of Education

One of the ongoing arguments throughout this text is that education should develop that which we consider most important about being human. Because each of the five philosophers discussed has a different version of what it means to be human, each has a different philosophy of education. The importance of determining what exemplifies being human will play a big role in our formulation of a philosophy of education.

FOUR FEATURES OF BEING HUMAN

Reason: We are capable of reason, and there are many practical advantages to critical and logical thinking. Yet there is a fear among some scholars that reason alone is insufficient, even dangerous, for it may become another form of authority and power used to manipulate, while not offering a superior truth, only a superior power. A large part of this debate is captured by the **modern** and **postmodern** conflict. Modernists believe reason is capable of saving humanity from its many vices, while some postmodernists see the use of reason as a dangerous vice. For our purposes, it is important to note that some philosophers have a very strong devotion to reason and also some who adamantly reject it as the key to being fully human.

Creativity: To create means to fashion or produce something new. This may mean using existing ideas and materials to create something that did not exist before, or it may mean coming up with an entirely new idea. We are capable of incredible creativity.

Emotion: We experience many different kinds of emotions, including happiness. As a species, we're generally interested in the pursuit of purpose, meaning, reason, and physical pleasures—among other things. These things foster happiness at an emotional and rational level. The tension between reason and emotion remains a major debate among many philosophers. Consider these four questions:

1. Should we exalt reason or emotion?
2. Are these separate, opposed, or connected to one another?
3. Should education help develop or foster our experience of the full range of human emotions?
4. Should it help us learn how to control certain emotions that might be damaging and to encourage emotions that are helpful to ourselves and others?

Our answers to these questions for a philosophy of education will be significant. In our culture, the techno-scientific seems to be very highly valued for its objective and rational character. Some have argued that science alone is capable of really revealing the world to us for it is not swayed or subject to human emotion and bias. Thus, for many people, the emotional side should be rejected as dangerous to our understanding of the world.

Freewill: In philosophy, you will find supporters situated all along a spectrum from hard determinism to complete freewill. This debate is often framed by the "nature or nurture" argument. **Determinism** states, generally, that we are biological creatures determined by our environments and physical nature. Humans are not free to make choices in a rational and objective manner—freewill is an illusion. While it may be important to live with the illusion of freewill, it is nevertheless a convenient fiction we create. Supporters of freewill believe that it is essential that humans learn how to make choices for themselves, for we create ourselves through our decisions—we are our choices. For supporters of freewill, a genuine education must be one in which individuals are encouraged to embrace their incredible responsibility.

WHY PHILOSOPHIZE ABOUT EDUCATION?

To philosophize about education is to systematically, in a rigorous and structured fashion, reflect upon the many activities and practices through which humans gain knowledge and understanding. It is through this investigation that many important theoretical and practical questions emerge that can be applied to future inquiries. By engaging with historically significant thinkers in the philosophical tradition, we become equipped to critically evaluate the sources and roles of education in our own lives, both as students and as teachers. If we reduce the aim of this book to one sentence, it would be to think critically and personally about the meaning of education. To ask "What is education?" (or "What does it mean?") seems like an obvious question, and yet the more we think about it the more difficult the answer seems. May we define education?

There are many things and experiences in life that reject simple definitions and explanations. Indeed a great deal of debate has taken place around this topic of defining education. Some argue that unless we may define it, clearly setting out necessary ideas and terms, we cannot hope to succeed at it. Others believe that we may only generalize about the topic of education, for there are simply too many forms and ideas within it to focus on a select few (and thereby privilege some ideas of education above others). Education is a vast topic that cannot be defined. If this is true, however, we need not give up before we begin. There is a great deal that may be said about education and learning without falling into either extreme of pursuing an exact definition or of living with pointless generalities. There are many different ways to do philosophy—to philosophize—and it will look different for everybody, but it will usually involve similar tools of critical reasoning, historical examination, and individual reflection.

Consider that compulsory education exists in many countries for those aged 6 to 16. It is law and social expectation that each citizen is educated under fairly specific criteria. I recall hearing about a local 14-year-old being arrested and put on probation for truancy—the illegal absence from compulsory education. To my knowledge, there were no other legal crimes, only the persistent absence from a recognized school.

The seriousness of avoiding formal schooling is certainly real. If one goes long enough without meeting educational expectations there will be social reprise, perhaps even legal punishment. The rationale often heard for this stance on compulsory education is that it is necessary for the adequate preparation of the young for their future. After all, if one cannot read and write, even the most basic jobs will be difficult.

We philosophize about education when we reflect on our convictions regarding expectations. Should we arrest, perhaps even forcibly institutionalize, those who opt out of education? How might we know when our best intentions have turned sour and our desire for enlightenment and job prospects have resulted in both real and proverbial captivity? Compulsory education precedes one's vocational choices, in effect opening up career avenues, but it also serves as a precondition for being an independent and responsible adult. Of course, many have had little or no formal education and have become responsible and successful adults. Regardless, many think of compulsory and formal education as a social rite of passage. It is commonplace to believe that children need to be educated for many years, even decades, but there are, in fact, many different reasons why education should take place. We will hear about many of these reasons from our five philosophers.

It is not enough that we know why we should invest in educating our young; we also need to decide what kind or form of education is best. Each of the five philosophers you will be introduced to in this book believes that the right form of education is essential to a prosperous and healthy society. Each believes that he has found a more comprehensive or proper way of thinking about education. And yet, most of their theories are either incompatible or contradictory when compared one to the other. For example, while Dewey envisions democracy as the key to education, Plato and Aristotle would strongly disagree. In fact, while there may be many features we like in each philosopher, it is unlikely that you will find the "right way" in any one philosophy, or perhaps even at all. Each proposal will have its merits and failings, which we must consider carefully in the creation of our personal philosophy of education.

Because education, whether formal or informal, is essential and integral to our maturation, it is important to question how our society has conceived and implemented educational institutions, and how adequately our approach to human development is being addressed. Each philosopher in this book will try to address such social and political questions in his own way. Moreover, before we begin to answer the how and why of educational theory, we must try to make sense of the more fundamental matters of what it means to be human. This too is something each philosopher in this book will examine thoroughly, all with very different conclusions. Indeed, as you are no doubt sensing by this point, this is a big-questions book.

CR

DISCUSSION QUESTIONS AND LEARNING ACTIVITIES

1. To what extent are you a philosopher? Which of the four main branches of philosophy do you feel most represents your approach?
2. What kind of truth claims do you tend to pay attention to: experience (your senses), faith, or reason?
3. What do you think are the defining features of being human? Rate the importance of logic, emotion, and intuition.
4. Why is the study of the philosophy of education important to you?
5. Do you think that religion and spirituality, like philosophy, art, ethics, and science, are fundamental aspects of human civilization that we cannot do without in education?
6. Upon what basis might you decide to opt out of an education?

Chapter 1

Plato

ଓ

The object of education is to teach us to love what is beautiful.
—Plato, *The Republic*

INTRODUCTION

In this chapter, you will be introduced to one of the greatest philosophers and thinkers of all time: Plato, who will challenge us to think of education in terms of social justice, harmony, and social well-being. Plato argues that our metaphysical understanding of reality must go beyond mere subjective opinion and social convention. Genuine education, for Plato, begins with thinking about life and seeking *the Good*—this requires an understanding of the individual, and to understand the individual we must look to the whole of society. If we accept Plato's assumption that we cannot know what good education is if we are ignorant of what makes a good society and a good person, then to develop a philosophy of education we must first develop a social and political philosophy.

We are beginning our inquiry into the philosophy of education with a thinker who lived over 2,000 years ago for a very good reason: Plato's influence is so great that it is difficult to measure. For example, the basic presuppositions of natural scientific methods are Platonic and Aristotelian, as are the philosophical presuppositions of Christianity. His ideas changed the intellectual landscape of the Western world.

Born sometime between 428 and 423 BCE, Plato was a philosopher and mathematician. In 387 BCE he founded the first institution of higher learning in the Western world: the Academy in Athens, Greece. Plato was a student of Socrates (470–399 BCE), and it is widely accepted that he wrote on his behalf. Many have questioned how accurate Plato's writings are to the historical person of Socrates, but though we may never know with certainty how much of Plato's dialogues reflect Socrates's philosophy, for our purposes, we will assume that Socrates's views are accurately expressed by Plato.

Plato is one of the most well-known and widely read philosophers of all time. Alfred North Whitehead, an influential 20th-century philosopher, once said that philosophy "consists of a series of footnotes to Plato" (*Process and Reality*, Free Press, 1979, p. 39). In other words, the very foundation for thinking (philosophically) in the Western world was laid by Plato. It would be almost impossible to give a list of philosophers that have their roots in Plato, for even those who reject his views must respond to them when attempting to create something new.

SOCRATES AND THE SOCRATIC METHOD

A central character throughout most of Plato's dialogues and a magnetic figure, Socrates is said to have been a heavy drinker and possessed the ability to meditate for long periods of time. The philosophies of Socrates, represented through the writing of Plato, put forward a peculiar kind of life. Socrates teaches his students to challenge assumptions, authority, and popular opinion—the good life, the happy life, begins by asking questions. Education begins in our ignorance, or rather our acknowledgment of ignorance, and the desire to find answers.

The Socratic Method starts when we try to identify our assumptions, and what is typically taken to be common sense, and then look for exceptions, refutations, or flaws in those beliefs. If we are sincere, we will likely find a great deal that is missing, incorrect, or simply meaningless. We must be wary of opinions, especially those not well thought through. No one has the right (something others are required to support) to blind opinion, according to Socrates, for that is merely dogmatic ignorance. For Socrates, rational non-conformity means being able to ask questions, no matter how unpopular the questions may be; working out what we really think; and then being able to stand behind your reasoned convictions. Socrates did not merely want to cause trouble; he wanted to find truth, the very meaning of life.

CONSIDER:

Do you see weakness in accepting truths without question?
What do you think are the dangers of conformity? How about non-conformity?
Do you agree with Socrates that human development and education rely on challenging the status quo?
Do you think it is important to explain your beliefs? Is that an essential ingredient to human development and education?

Socrates's Ethical Rationalism

Perhaps best known for developing an ethical rationalism, Socrates argues that ethical truths are rational and teachable, not relative. He objects to ethical relativism in which one might say "I am the ultimate judge of right and wrong." Merely because one believes that he or she is right does not necessarily make it so. A key part of his philosophy is the belief that *good* people will act *good*—to know good is to do good.

Knowing the right thing and then being able to do it is far from simple. For Socrates, the practical know-how of poets, craftsmen, farmers, and labourers is of little use when it comes to knowing true beauty and the Good (the highest knowledge or truth). Being able to plough a field is a kind of good, but it is a far cry from the most good—

the *ideal* good. The theoretical knowledge of scientists, engineers, and technicians is of little use when it comes to living nobly and justly by participating in the Good. While it may be interesting and helpful to know the structure of an atom, this knowledge does not really help one realize potential as a human being. Knowing facts and data about the world may be useful, but such facts do not of themselves lead us toward becoming better people. The wisdom and self-reflection needed to attain the good life belongs to philosophers. Philosophers are those who think about life, its meaning and purpose, and who continually question and challenge dogmatic assumptions and beliefs.

DIALOGUE CONCERNING KNOWLEDGE AND PERCEPTION, FROM *THEAETETUS*

Socrates: A question which I think that you must often have heard persons ask:-How can you determine whether at this moment we are sleeping, and all our thoughts are a dream; or whether we are awake, and talking to one another in the waking state?

Theaetetus: Indeed, Socrates, I do not know how to prove the one any more than the other, for in both cases the facts precisely correspond;-and there is no difficulty in supposing that during all this discussion we have been talking to one another in a dream; and when in a dream we seem to be narrating dreams, the resemblance of the two states is quite astonishing.

Socrates: You see, then, that a doubt about the reality of sense is easily raised, since there may even be a doubt whether we are awake or in a dream. And as our time is equally divided between sleeping and waking, in either sphere of existence the soul contends that the thoughts which are present to our minds at the time are true; and during one half of our lives we affirm the truth of the one, and, during the other half, of the other; and are equally confident of both.

Theaetetus: Most true.

Socrates: And may not the same be said of madness and other disorders? the difference is only that the times are not equal.

Theaetetus: Certainly.

Socrates: And is truth or falsehood to be determined by duration of time?

Theaetetus: That would be in many ways ridiculous.

Socrates: But can you certainly determine: by any other means which of these opinions is true?

Theaetetus: I do not think that I can.

Socrates: Listen, then, to a statement of the other side of the argument, which is made by the champions of appearance. They would say, as I imagine-can that which is wholly other than something, have the same quality as that from which it differs? and observe, -Theaetetus, that the word "other" means not "partially," but "wholly other."

Theaetetus: Certainly, putting the question as you do, that which is wholly other cannot either potentially or in any other way be the same.

Socrates: And must therefore be admitted to be unlike?

Theaetetus: True.

Socrates: If, then, anything happens to become like or unlike itself or another, when it becomes like we call it the same-when unlike, other?

Theaetetus: Certainly.

Socrates: Were we not saying that there are agents many and infinite, and patients many and infinite?

Theaetetus: Yes.

Socrates: And also that different combinations will produce results which are not the same, but different?

Theaetetus: Certainly.

Socrates: Let us take you and me, or anything as an example:-There is Socrates in health, and Socrates sick-Are they like or unlike?

Theaetetus: You mean to, compare Socrates in health as a whole, and Socrates in sickness as a whole?

Socrates: Exactly; that is my meaning.

Theaetetus: I answer, they are unlike.

Socrates: And if unlike, they are other?

Theaetetus: Certainly.

Socrates: And would you not say the same of Socrates sleeping and waking, or in any of the states which we were mentioning?

Theaetetus: I should.

Socrates: All agents have a different patient in Socrates, accordingly as he is well or ill.

Theaetetus: Of course.

Socrates: And I who am the patient, and that which is the agent, will produce something different in each of the two cases?

Theaetetus: Certainly.

Socrates: The wine which I drink when I am in health, appears sweet and pleasant to me?

Theaetetus: True.

Socrates: For, as has been already acknowledged, the patient and agent meet together and produce sweetness and a perception of sweetness, which are in simultaneous motion, and the perception which comes from the patient makes the tongue percipient, and the quality of sweetness which arises out of and is moving about the wine, makes the wine, both to be and to appear sweet to the healthy tongue.

Theaetetus: Certainly; that has been already acknowledged.

Socrates: But when I am sick, the wine really acts upon another and a different person?

Theaetetus: Yes.

Socrates: The combination of the draught of wine, and the Socrates who is sick, produces quite another result; which is the sensation of bitterness in the tongue, and the, motion and creation of bitterness in and about the wine, which becomes not bitterness but something bitter; as I myself become not but percipient?

Theaetetus: True.

Socrates: There is no, other object of which I shall ever have the same perception, for another object would give another perception, and would make the perception other and different; nor can that object which affects me, meeting another, subject, produce, the same, or become similar, for that too would produce another result from another subject, and become different.

Theaetetus: True.

Socrates: Neither can by myself, have this sensation, nor the object by itself, this quality.

Theaetetus: Certainly not.

Socrates: When I perceive I must become percipient of something-there can be no such thing as perceiving and perceiving nothing; the object, whether it become sweet, bitter, or of any other quality, must have relation to a percipient; nothing can become sweet which is sweet to no one.

Theaetetus: Certainly not.

Socrates: Then the inference is, that we [the agent and patient] are or become in relation to one another; there is a law which binds us one to the other, but not to any other existence, nor each of us to himself; and therefore we can only be bound to one another; so that whether a person says that a thing is or becomes, he must say that it is or becomes to or of or in relation to something else; but he must not say or allow any one else to say that anything is or becomes absolutely: -such is our conclusion.

Theaetetus: Very true, Socrates.

Socrates: Then, if that which acts upon me has relation to me and to no other, I and no other am the percipient of it?

Theaetetus: Of course.

Socrates: Then my perception is true to me, being inseparable from my own being; and, as Protagoras says, to myself I am judge of what is and-what is not to me.

Theaetetus: I suppose so.

Socrates: How then, if I never err, and if my mind never trips in the conception of being or becoming, can I fail of knowing that which I perceive?

Theaetetus: You cannot.

Socrates: Then you were quite right in affirming that knowledge is only perception; and the meaning turns out to be the same, whether with Homer and Heracleitus, and all that company, you say that all is motion and flux, or with the great sage Protagoras, that man is the measure of all things; or with Theaetetus, that, given these premises, perception is knowledge. Am I not right, Theaetetus, and is not this your newborn child, of which I have delivered you? What say you?

Theaetetus: I cannot but agree, Socrates.

Socrates: Then this is the child, however he may turn out, which you and I have with difficulty brought into the world. And now that he is born, we must run round the hearth with him, and see whether he is worth rearing, or is only a wind-egg and a sham. Is he to be reared in any case, and not exposed?

or will you bear to see him rejected, and not get into a passion if I take away your first-born?

Theodorus: Theaetetus will not be angry, for he is very good-natured. But tell me, Socrates, in heaven's name, is this, after all, not the truth?

Socrates: You, Theodorus, are a lover of theories, and now you innocently fancy that I am a bag full of them, and can easily pull one out which will overthrow its predecessor. But you do not see that in reality none of these theories come from me; they all come from him who talks with me. I only know just enough to extract them from the wisdom of another, and to receive them in a spirit of fairness. And now I shall say nothing myself, but shall endeavour to elicit something from our young friend.

Theodorus: Do as you say, Socrates; you are quite right.

SOCRATES'S PHILOSOPHY: THE UNEXAMINED LIFE IS NOT WORTH LIVING
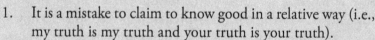

1. It is a mistake to claim to know good in a relative way (i.e., my truth is my truth and your truth is your truth).
2. It is contradictory to claim to know the good or right thing and then not carry it out.
3. It is contradictory to claim to live a life worth living if one avoids examining and reflecting upon it sincerely and deeply.

To be a genuine philosopher, according to Socrates, one must know the Good; this is possible by seeking the Good through contemplation and radical questioning. Seeking the Good requires a great deal

Foundations of Education

of effort, time, sincerity, frustration, and self-sacrifice. Once one has worked hard to understand what is good—one must do good; otherwise, it will be evident that the philosopher has failed to learn what is truly good. Socrates claimed that if we do these things we will have a chance at a happy and successful life, albeit an unusual life that defines success and happiness in uncommon, perhaps even counterintuitive, ways. Socrates's philosophy encourages a kind of ignorance; for example, after speaking to a politician he thinks to himself:

> I am wiser than this man; it is likely that neither of us knows anything worthwhile, but he thinks he knows something when he does not, whereas I do not know, neither do I think I know; so I am likely to be wiser than he to this small extent, that I do not think I know what I do not know. (*Apology* 21d)

For Socrates, true understanding, knowledge, and a life worth living begins with the recognition of our ignorance. The good life begins by accepting that we do not know.

It is important to point out that Socrates did not expect his philosophies to be adopted by all, rather only a rare select few could truly benefit from his tutelage. Additionally, many would-be philosophers have neither the time nor money to invest in serious philosophical study—this is as true today as it was in Socrates's time; furthermore, presuming time and money are not barriers, it is not clear immediately what Socrates promises his devout philosophers. Is ignorance the goal or merely the starting point for genuine discovery?

PLATO'S UNIVERSAL TRUTHS AND IDEALISM

Plato, like many Ancient Greek thinkers, was worried about change, motion, diversity, or flux. He wanted to find some way to come to intellectual and emotional grips with the strange world in which we live. Moreover, he wanted to find a handle, key, or lever—metaphorically speaking—that could be used to comprehend and make sense of human experience. For Plato, and many other thinkers of that time, the answer lay beyond the material world in principles, laws, and universal ideas.

The first 30 years of Plato's life were filled with war, leaving him consumed with ideas of harmony and unity, which may have lead to his development of **Platonism**. Plato's contributions to Western thought include his theories on metaphysics, epistemology, and ethics—he is widely considered one of the most influential people of all time. Of course, this does not mean that his views are widely accepted as true, only that his philosophy sparked revolutions of new thought and reflection. Like Socrates, Plato sought universals—absolute and objective truths that exist outside of our minds—through which we may not only describe the universe but also prescribe proper thought and action. Here is a brief summary of Plato's famous argument regarding the *most real* reality:

1. There is something independent of all things, for it depends upon nothing else for its existence.
2. There is something absolute that does not come into being or go out of being, or change in any way.
3. These facts point to a world of reality (Being), beyond our world of becoming (change, corruption, and decay).
4. The world of Being is populated by non-visible Forms.
5. A Form is the essence, nature, or essential structure of a thing.
6. What a thing is, its *whatness*, is caused by these invisible Forms.
7. Forms are eternal, transcendent, nonsensical—only known by the intellect, perfect, and archetypal—for they are models for everything that does or could exist.
8. Above all things is the Form of the Good.

In short, Plato concludes that true reality, the *most real* reality, is the Form of the Good. He believes that if we set our sights and souls on attaining this kind of truth then we will have the best form of a philosophy of education. All other goals are inferior, though perhaps important in their own right.

Plato's metaphysics relies on a dualism, the division of soul (Form) from body (material content) and the division between this world (comprised of that which changes and corrupts) and the realm of absolute (objective Forms and ideas). The good life is possible only when we are able to recognize these features of reality and ourselves. Once we are oriented toward true reality we will be able to foster justice and harmony in ourselves and in our societies. It is only when we are attuned to this reality that we are able to say we are progressing in our education.

CONSIDER:

Are there fixed rules, universal laws, or principles through which we might construct a universal philosophy of education?

Is there such thing as immorality, or is morality merely a social convention?

Is there a universal good for all people, across all cultures, across all time? If not, are we left with moral relativism?

Do you agree that we must get in touch with a greater reality if we are to progress as an individual? How about as a society?

What are your thoughts on dualism? Are our minds and souls united or separate?

Figure 1.1 is a graphical representation of Plato's famous argument of the Divided Line in Book VI of *The Republic*. The diagram is meant to give us a general idea of the different levels and hierarchies of reality and being that Plato discusses.

This diagram depicts an intelligible world at the top and a world of appearances at the bottom. Represented at the top is what we know by virtue of our souls, a higher or greater reality, whereas the bottom is the visible world, what we perceive in our ordinary lives. That is not the most real reality, as it is deceptive and always incomplete.

It is very strange for us, as modern thinkers, to appreciate Plato situating what we know empirically (that which we perceive through our senses) as lower forms of reality while the soul

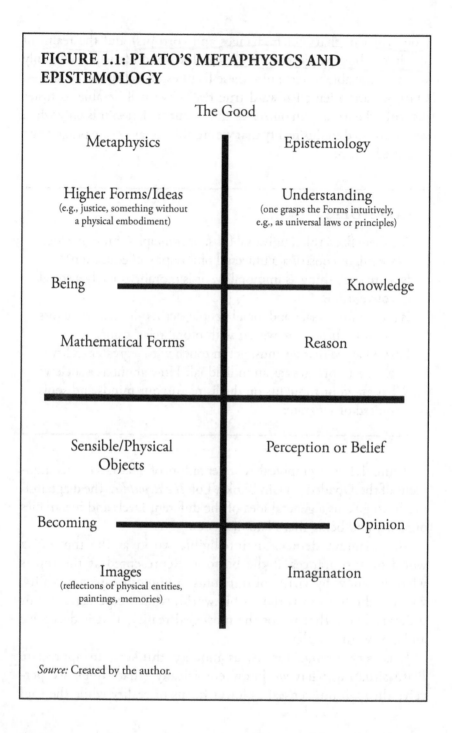

FIGURE 1.1: PLATO'S METAPHYSICS AND EPISTEMOLOGY

The Good

Metaphysics

Epistemiology

Higher Forms/Ideas
(e.g., justice, something without
a physical embodiment)

Understanding
(one grasps the Forms intuitively,
e.g., as universal laws or principles)

Being

Knowledge

Mathematical Forms

Reason

Sensible/Physical
Objects

Perception or Belief

Becoming

Opinion

Images
(reflections of physical entities,
paintings, memories)

Imagination

Source: Created by the author.

or mind (ideas) are said to better grasp Being (truth/reality). We are accustomed to scientific notions of truth and objectivity—for something to be a reliable fact it should be something we can hear, see, taste, touch, or smell; proof and evidence are usually required if we are to believe in something's existence. Plato's proof is not something that can be weighed, measured, or seen with the naked eye. What is really objective and true may only be known by the rational part of the soul. Plato argues that the lowest of things are images and shadows of reality—shadows of the Good—as the Good cannot be found or measured in this world of imperfect and changing things. We must move beyond the world of mere belief and opinion toward a more perfect and unchanging reality; it is this reality that will be the basis of all knowledge and under-standing—education.

There are many different levels of Being (or reality), and all things in the world have Being of some kind. For instance, the immutable divine (an unchanging God) has more Being than a goldfish or a tree. The higher up Plato's hierarchy we go the more Being something has. For example, if I want to understand a maple leaf I will find one on a tree or on the ground and I will examine it with my senses. Plato tells us that such an examination is of an imperfect specimen. This leaf is probably partially eaten by bugs, perhaps it is changing colour for fall, or maybe it is in perfect health and shape but it is from a young tree. Whatever this particular leaf is, it is only a shadow of perfect *maple-leafness*—the ideal perfect and unchanging form of all maple leaves that exists invisibly behind all that we see.

The Allegory of the Cave

Plato's allegory of the cave in Book VII of *The Republic* is one of his most famous contributions to philosophy. It is a device, or story, meant to make the theory of Forms more accessible and understandable. It establishes two worlds: a world of appearances and the real world.

THE ALLEGORY OF THE CAVE: A CONVERSATION BETWEEN SOCRATES AND GLAUCON, FROM *THE REPUBLIC*

And now, I said, let me show in a figure how far our nature is enlightened or unenlightened—Behold! Human beings living in an underground den, which has a mouth open toward the light and reaching all along the den; here they have been from their childhood, and have their legs and necks chained so that they cannot move, and can only see before them, being prevented by the chains from turning round their heads. Above and behind them a fire is blazing at a distance, and between the fire and the prisoners there is a raised way; and you will see, if you look, a low wall built along the way, like the screen which marionette players have in front of them, over which they show the puppets.

I see.

And do you see, I said, men passing along the wall carrying all sorts of vessels, and statues and figures of animals made of wood and stone and various materials, which appear over the wall? Some of them are talking, others silent.

You have shown me a strange image, and they are strange prisoners.

Like ourselves, I replied; and they see only their own shadows, or the shadows of one another, which the fire throws on the opposite wall of the cave?

True, he said; how could they see anything but the shadows if they were never allowed to move their heads?

And of the objects which are being carried in like manner they would only see the shadows?

Yes, he said.

And if they were able to converse with one another, would they not suppose that they were naming what was actually before them?

Very true.

And suppose further that the prison had an echo which came from the other side, would they not be sure to fancy when one of the passers-by spoke that the voice which they heard came from the passing shadow?

No question, he replied.

To them, I said, the truth would be literally nothing but the shadows of the images.

That is certain.

And now look again, and see what will naturally follow it—the prisoners are released and disabused of their error. At first, when any of them is liberated and compelled suddenly to stand up and turn his neck round and walk and look toward the light, he will suffer sharp pains; the glare will distress him, and he will be unable to see the realities of which in his former state he had seen the shadows; and then conceive someone saying to him, that what he saw before was an illusion, but that now, when he is approaching nearer to being and his eye is turned toward more real existence, he has a clearer vision—what will be his reply? And you may further imagine that his instructor is pointing to the objects as they pass and requiring him to name them—will he not be perplexed? Will he not fancy that the shadows which he formerly saw are truer than the objects which are now shown to him?

Far truer.

And if he is compelled to look straight at the light, will he not have a pain in his eyes which will make him turn away to take and take in the objects of vision which he can see, and which he will conceive to be in reality clearer than the things which are now being shown to him?

True, he now.

And suppose once more, that he is reluctantly dragged up a steep and rugged ascent, and held fast until he's forced into the presence of the sun himself, is he not likely to be pained and irritated? When he approaches the light his eyes will be dazzled, and he will not be able to see anything at all of what are now called realities.

Not all in a moment, he said.

He will require to grow accustomed to the sight of the upper world. And first he will see the shadows best, next the reflections of men and other objects in the water, and then the objects themselves; then he will gaze upon the light of the moon and the stars and the spangled heaven; and he will see the sky and the stars by night better than the sun or the light of the sun by day?

Certainly.

Last of he will be able to see the sun, and not mere reflections of him in the water, but he will see him in his own proper place, and not in another; and he will contemplate him as he is.

Certainly.

He will then proceed to argue that this is he who gives the season and the years, and is the guardian of all that is in the visible world, and in a certain way the cause of all things which he and his fellows have been accustomed to behold?

Clearly, he said, he would first see the sun and then reason about him.

And when he remembered his old habitation, and the wisdom of the den and his fellow-prisoners, do you not suppose that he would felicitate himself on the change, and pity them?

Certainly, he would.

And if they were in the habit of conferring honours among themselves on those who were quickest to observe the passing shadows and to remark which of them went before, and which followed after, and which were together; and who were therefore best able to draw conclusions as to the future, do you think that he would care for such honours and glories, or envy the possessors of them? Would he not say with Homer: Better to be the poor servant of a poor master, and to endure anything, rather than think as they do and live after their manner?

Yes, he said, I think that he would rather suffer anything than entertain these false notions and live in this miserable manner.

In the allegory, the cave stands for the visible world and the fire stands for the power of the Sun in the outside world that makes everything visible. The Sun is the symbol of the Form of the Good, toward which every Form is oriented—every essence within everything, including each of us. Most humans dwell in the darkness of the cave; however, some of us, especially philosophers, may move from within the cave to the outside. This movement is one in which the soul becomes closer to the intelligible—the most real, the realm of Forms. Such a journey, for Plato, may be achieved in large part through a proper education. However, education does not consist in putting knowledge into the soul or mind. Rather, it is about turning the eyes of the soul toward the Good. One may be educated in so much as the soul is correctly directed, not instructed with facts or information. The capacity to see the truth is available to all, but according to Plato, most of us will avoid the pain of looking into the light. Instead, many prefer to live in the cave, with dimly lit shadows as our reality.

CONSIDER:

Is the role of a teacher to force their students to look at the truth? Must a good education force us to face realities that are painful and difficult?

Perhaps a good teacher is one who does not force but entices students to look toward truth. Plato's philosophers cannot force anyone toward truth; consider the efficacy of the Socratic Method in getting people to rethink their beliefs.

Three Classes of People: Philosopher Kings, Auxiliaries (Guardians), and the Masses

Plato believes that society is comprised of three parts and that people are by nature suited for one and only one of the three groups. Plato so strongly believed this that he proposed a "noble lie" meant to convince each of us of our proper place. The lie encourages each person to accept that the gods had chosen our destiny: some of us are made of gold, while others are made of silver, bronze, or iron. Education reveals what we are made up of as well as our proper class.

Plato identified philosopher kings as the highest level of attainment, followed by the guardian class, while the masses occupy the lowest class.

The basic principle of a well-organized society is that each of us should concentrate on what we are supposed to do, what we each do best. In other words, a harmonious society is one in which individuals know their respective places and each person stays correctly situated.

PLATO'S THREE CLASSES

1. Rulers or **philosopher kings** are tested throughout their lives to see whether their judgment is affected by the hardships they face or if they are capable of keeping on the right path despite their difficulties. In order to become philosopher kings, guardians must undergo a long and intense process of education. Students are to remain at home, where they can receive a moral education until age 7, then be trained in music and sport until age 17. From 18 to 20 they receive physical training and do military service, and from 20 to 30 they learn mathematics, including geometry, calculus, and arithmetic. From 30 to 35 they study dialectic and pure theory about ultimate principles of reality, and from 35 to 50 they gain practical experience by taking office in the government, perhaps even taking command in war. Finally, at age 50, the students that have succeeded long enough will be ready to live lives of philosophical contemplation of the Good and, when needed, to assume the role of philosopher king.

2. The **auxiliaries** or **guards** assist the rulers by enforcing their rule. Think of this category as the police officers who execute the will of the law. Auxiliary guardians are under strict prohibition from owning private property and making money. Plato believes that the city should provide a modest salary for them by way of taxation from the rest of society. However, in Plato's *Republic*, Adeimantus argues that such auxiliaries look like paid mercenaries who would not have much incentive to do their job. The reply is that the aim of the just city is not the happiness of the auxiliaries but the happiness of all. Plato argues that they must be spared the tasks that threaten to corrupt them the most—money-making and land ownership.

3. The **masses** are made up of everyone else in society: the money-makers and workers, including artists and farmers. The masses do not have access to full knowledge. This does not mean that such members of society cannot be good, only that they cannot participate in the Form of the Good like philosopher kings.

The conflict in Plato's thinking between concern for the state and concern for the individual is striking. He wants to allow each individual to become whatever one is capable of being, but he does not want anyone to think more highly of himself than appropriate. A guardian who has failed to prove himself worthy of becoming a philosopher king should not continue to insist that he may achieve such a status—his role is to support the philosopher king. Moreover, a farmer will be less happy in life if he continues to think of himself as a one-day guardian. If you are a member of the masses but you act as if you are a philosopher king or ruler you will be fostering disharmony in yourself and your society. According to Plato, we are made with certain capacities and natures that education reveals. As demonstrated by the rigorous system of education for philosopher kings, Plato takes human education and development very seriously—there is a lot to learn and it takes time to learn it. Moreover, learning goes beyond facts and requires lived experience.

CONSIDER:

Do you believe that it is acceptable to require that people fit into predetermined places within society?

Why would these designations help make society more harmonious?

What are your thoughts on Plato's tiers of education? How do these compare to the tiers of contemporary education?

Do you think it's possible to be motivated to serve society, despite being denied property and wealth?

As a whole, all three categories of people constitute one entity, a **polity**, and it is this entity that seeks harmony, justice, and knowledge.

Justice: The Just Person and the Just City

Justice, the good life, and education go hand-in-hand for Plato. Justice can be described as the quality of giving each person their due—if someone does good, then they deserve good done to them; if bad, then bad. Alternately, justice is said to be in the possession of superior power—the most powerful person will always be in charge, whether we like it or not, and will determine what justice is. Plato's Socrates rejects both options: real justice never involves harming another, and good conduct does not mean acting in self-interest.

Justice is one of the four cardinal virtues, which were developed in Plato's discussion of the just city in *The Republic*. He argues that we will have a good, just, and harmonious city when the other three virtues—moderation, courage, and wisdom or prudence—are active.

Plato argues that we should only educate those with good moral character; students with bad moral character should be excluded. This might seem strange, as most industrialized nations foster inclusive education regardless of moral character, but we may clarify Plato's point simply by using the catchphrase "knowledge is power." Education is an incredibly powerful tool that might be disastrous in the wrong hands.

CONSIDER:

Do you think it would ever be a good idea to keep education from some people?

Do you think Plato's standards of justice are attainable?

What do you think of our political leaders today? Have they been sufficiently educated in a manner worthy of Plato?

Morality, character, and education are inseparable for Plato. In Plato's city we find wisdom to be the virtue of the philosopher king, courage as the virtue of guardians, and moderation as the virtue of the masses. Justice, for Plato, is to be found in the attribute or character of the city that allows for these qualities to come to the fore. This is so because justice produces harmony; it is the result of control and the correct performance of one's task in respect to their class.

Plato argues that in the same way that there are three classes of people in the city, the soul of each individual also consists of three parts:

1. The calculating or rational part that knows what ought to be and how we ought to act—characteristic of the philosopher kings.
2. The spirited part enforces how we behave—personified by the guardians.
3. The desiring or the appetitive part is our raw instinctual impulse—hallmarked by the masses.

Relying on this analogy, if the same three virtues are properly ordered in the individual's soul, then that person would be a just person, like the same virtues in a city would make it a just city. Justice within an individual means that one does not allow himself to mind other people's business (each should fulfill his own natural place) and one does not let the parts of the soul meddle with each other (each should fulfill its own function). Plato is emphatic that reason should rule the soul as only it has access to the Form of the Good. The philosopher's journey is toward truth, and his obligation is to return and live it out as an example to others.

What sets Plato apart from many early philosophers is his belief in sexual equality: women should be given the same education as men in order to perform the same tasks. While some might object that such education would be contrary to custom, Plato responds by arguing that while society may ridicule those who do not follow custom, it is not a good reason to conform to social pressure. Plato acknowledges that some believe that men and women are by nature different—to this he responds that such differences are superficial like those between a bald and a long-haired man. Plato is a radical thinker in this regard; in the next chapter we will turn to Aristotle and explore why he thinks Plato is wrong. Essentially, Aristotle believes that it is unfair to expect women to be able to perform in the same manner as men because they are inherently different, and therefore their educational experiences should also be different.

Plato strongly believes in justice but rejects democracy as the natural and proper outcome of a good education. He argues that because it is possible to construct the ideal city in theory and because theory has a higher status than the everyday world of appearances (which is comprised of that which changes, corrupts, and decays) then it should be possible to achieve theory in reality. As we have briefly touched on, the foremost change needed in existing cities to enable them to be governed justly is for them to be ruled by philosophers. As to the question of what it is that qualifies philosophers more than anyone else to rule and educate, Plato answers this by saying that it is their ability to access and know true reality, the Forms.

Plato rejects the democratic form in which all people rule, even the poor, because democracy does not have an objective standard of value. It does not require that we follow reason, leaving us to be irrational and motivated by fear. This ultimately leads to prioritizing self-interest, which is not good for oneself or one's society. Moreover, democracy seems to allow for the ignorant to rule. There are no safeguards in democracy to prevent the least informed and self-controlled from steering the whole proverbial ship. He also rejects oligarchy, in which a few elites rule. His conclusion is that both options exploit and mistake what is really good; ultimately, both will devolve into tyranny. To avoid exploitation we must have reason as our goal. We must love truth and knowledge over lust and greed. Philosopher kings are our proper rulers not because they want to rule, but because they want to rule the least—they are the least self-interested among us and therefore the least likely to take advantage of others.

CHALLENGES TO THE PHILOSOPHIES OF PLATO AND SOCRATES

The notion that we ought to privilege philosophical education as uniquely suited to yielding a good society has been met with harsh criticism. One such criticism is that philosophers seem to be functionally irrelevant, in that they spend so much time thinking that they scarcely have the ability to be practical and actually run society. Plato acknowledges that in his own time philosophers have been isolated by society; regardless, they are best suited to rule if we give them a chance and we will see that they are exceptionally capable and practical.

Another popular criticism lobbied against Plato is that his philosophy is ultimately in support of tyrants and dictators. There is a totalitarian feel to Plato's just city according to some scholars, such as Karl Popper, the famous philosopher of science. Indeed, Plato does argue that we must control and censor what some people see and do, but he also argues that we must treat people carefully. Because people are susceptible to negative influences, they must be protected (via censors and lies) from such influences and even from their own misguided passions and desires, similar to the way that children should be protected against certain ideas until they are old enough to understand and critically judge mature concepts.

Another significant set of criticism stem from the parallels between Plato's philosophy and National Socialism (Nazism) in terms of (1) eugenics, or selective breeding; (2) a hierarchical society in which some are superior to others, including one ruler over many; and (3) political domination and control over the lives of people. In fact, Plato does encourage a kind of eugenics (the intentional change of a genetic population), although his is not a biological kind. For instance, Plato argues that those who possess higher faculties of mind (virtue) and a proven love of the city ought to be responsible for child rearing. Plato fosters a hierarchical society in which others must submit to the ruler, but such a hierarchy is not for the sake of the ruler. According to Plato, people will be miserable if they are not governed correctly. Submitting is for our benefit—that is, our liberty is limited for our benefit. The ideal for Plato is not political control, but self-control. When self-control fails (as it seems to), we need political control.

PLATO'S PHILOSOPHY OF EDUCATION

Plato's argument is that we cannot know what a good education will
look like if we are ignorant of what makes a good society and a good
individual, and these, of course, are connected to our metaphysical understandings. To develop a philosophy of education we must
develop a political philosophy, an epistemology, and an ethics; to
ground these things we must have a robust metaphysics. Plato's concepts of justice, harmony, virtue, and the Good are far from clear
or straightforward. Yet, his ethical rationalism remains an important
source of inspiration to many modern theories of social justice and
education, even though these newer theories might not take his metaphysical views to heart. It is not surprising that most contemporary
philosophers reject Plato's metaphysics; however, many of his basic
strategies for making sense of knowledge and truth remain popular,
especially the pursuit of a foundation, principles, and laws.

ଓ

DISCUSSION QUESTIONS
AND LEARNING ACTIVITIES

1. Build an education ladder, similar to Plato's Metaphysics and Epistemology diagram, that includes all of the subjects that you believe are important—with the most important at the top and the least important at the bottom. Ultimately your goal is to provide the best education possible, so that students are likely to become healthy and contributing members of society.
   a) In addition to topics, try to identify specific skills that an ideal educational experience should include.
   b) Consider how long it would take to become a healthy functioning adult according to your ladder.
   c) By what standard or value do you determine good, better, or best goals?
   d) Consider why you have given higher priority to some things and not others.
2. Try to answer the following questions in the context of this chapter:
   a) What is a philosopher?
   b) What should the pursuit of knowledge look like according to Plato?
   c) What, for Plato, should the purpose of government be in relation to education?
   d) Do you believe that governments should be responsible for educating citizens on truth and morality or is the ownership and control of education better left in private hands?
   e) Do you believe that education ought to seek an understanding of what is universal, absolute, and unchanging?

Chapter 2

Aristotle

ℭℛ

All men by nature desire to know. An indication of this is the delight we take in our senses; for even apart from their usefulness they are loved for themselves; and above all others the sense of sight. For not only with a view to action, but even when we are not going to do anything, we prefer seeing (one might say) to everything else. The reason is that this, most of all the senses, makes us know....

—Aristotle, *Metaphysics*

INTRODUCTION

Education is at the very heart of Aristotle's philosophy. He argues that it helps humans achieve their greatest potential and, ultimately, happiness. For Aristotle, human excellence is not merely personal; it is only possible in a social context. In this chapter, we will consider some of the major differences between Plato and Aristotle and the significance of developing a philosophy of education in light of human nature, specifically our political and social nature. Most readers will need to read Aristotle's work more than once due to his dry style and sheer depth of intellect. Like Plato, his influence has reached far and wide in both the fields he contributed to and those which emerged from his achievements. Even by today's standards, Aristotle's interests seem virtually limitless. His writings cover a vast range of topics across the human, social, and natural sciences. He is credited with inventing the sciences of logic, physics, zoology, and botany, and for coining the term *metaphysics*. His legacy is in many respects a fulfillment of what Plato and Socrates began, namely, to set the foundations for modern science and philosophy.

Born in 384 BCE, Aristotle attended the Academy in Athens where he was a student of Plato. When Plato died in 347 BCE, Aristotle left the Academy and Athens after not being appointed to fill Plato's position. He eventually returned in 334 or 335 BCE to establish a school at the Lyceum.

MAJOR DIFFERENCES BETWEEN THE PHILOSOPHIES OF PLATO AND ARISTOTLE

1. Plato argues that the best educated among us should lead us as philosopher kings or queens, whereas Aristotle argues that having philosophers as rulers will lead to an abuse of power and ultimately to tyrannical rule. Also, because women lack the ability to reason effectively, Aristotle thinks they would make terrible rulers.

2. Aristotle argues that Plato is wrong to dismantle institutions of family and private property, as he did for the auxiliary class. These are natural and desirable, as both contribute to the happiness of citizens. Moreover, family promotes virtue—without family and property Aristotle thinks they would be living unnatural and miserable lives. In short, the desire to own property and have a family is a good thing in moderation. Aristotle argues that even philosophers would eventually end up being unhappy in Plato's ideal society.

3. Aristotle's approach is typified by observation and description in which the good or best way to think about one's life (its purpose, etc.) is to rely on what is in nature. Plato does not do this because he relies on a transcendental world of Forms known through reason.

4. Aristotle's heightened sense of practical reasonableness is contrasted with Plato's prescriptive philosophy aimed at

a heavenly realm. Plato does not seem to recognize the practical realities we experience to the same degree of Aristotle's philosophy. For example, an important theme in Aristotle's philosophy argues that we ought to strive for a **golden mean** (a mean between extremes) in our daily actions.

5. According to Aristotle, Plato does not understand human nature, so he cannot offer strong grounds for creating an efficient society. Ultimately, Plato's polity will end with corruption, as he has failed to find a descriptive and realistic view of power. True governments govern with an eye toward the common good. Aristotle believes that the ideal society will be ruled by the middle class, as it represents moderation.

6. Both philosophers' understandings of politics rely heavily on metaphysics; however, Aristotle's position is more ethically driven. Aristotle is concerned with the good that we may attain through action, which is dependent on our purpose, end, or intention.

METAPHYSICS

Both Plato and Aristotle ground their respective philosophies of education in metaphysics, and yet the results are very different. For instance, Aristotle rejects Plato's separation of reality and argues that our concern should be this world of changing things, not some unknown heavenly realm. We must, according to Aristotle, begin our investigation in the sensed world. Though Aristotle was tremendously influenced by Plato, and they agree that there must be some underlying Form—some kind of essence to all things that makes them what they are—their versions are very different. Like Plato, Aristotle believes that it is through Forms (the objective essences of things) that we can make sense of the order around us (e.g., nature, morality, and politics). Unlike Plato, Aristotle's Forms are immanent in particular things. Like Plato, Aristotle is concerned with change: to understand the world of change we must find that thing that is unchanging, that thing that accounts for the stability of reality. Unlike Plato, Aristotle is not concerned with *this-ness*, the universal *orangeness* or *tableness* of things—the hidden ideals behind all things—but specific tables and an actual orange. Aristotle argues that it is the Form (the essence or *whatness* of a thing) along with matter (a concrete expression of a thing) that makes it real—therefore no ideal reality or separate Forms are needed.

One important consensus between Plato and Aristotle is that the universe is a rational and structured thing that may be known, if we are able to figure out its foundation and rational nature. It is also important to note that the belief that the universe is knowable, rational, and structured is not a universally held view; nor is the belief that a philosophy of education should inform us of such things. Aristotle's approach to the universe is scientific by contemporary standards. The scientific approach is so widely accepted by modern societies that many of us do not stop to question it.

FROM *METAPHYSICS, BOOK I*

The animals other than man live by appearances and memories, and have but little of connected experience; but the human race lives also by art and reasonings. Now from memory experience is produced in men; for the several memories of the same thing produce finally the capacity for a single experience. And experience seems pretty much like science and art, but really science and art come to men through experience; for 'experience made art', as Polus says, 'but inexperience luck.' Now art arises when from many notions gained by experience one universal judgement about a class of objects is produced. For to have a judgement that when Callias was ill of this disease this did him good, and similarly in the case of Socrates and in many individual cases, is a matter of experience; but to judge that it has done good to all persons of a certain constitution, marked off in one class, when they were ill of this disease, e.g.

Foundations of Education

to phlegmatic or bilious people when burning with fevers-this is a matter of art.

With a view to action experience seems in no respect inferior to art, and men of experience succeed even better than those who have theory without experience. (The reason is that experience is knowledge of individuals, art of universals, and actions and productions are all concerned with the individual; for the physician does not cure man, except in an incidental way, but Callias or Socrates or some other called by some such individual name, who happens to be a man. If, then, a man has the theory without the experience, and recognizes the universal but does not know the individual included in this, he will often fail to cure; for it is the individual that is to be cured.) But yet we think that knowledge and understanding belong to art rather than to experience, and we suppose artists to be wiser than men of experience (which implies that Wisdom depends in all cases rather on knowledge); and this because the former know the cause, but the latter do not. For men of experience know that the thing is so, but do not know why, while the others know the 'why' and the cause. Hence we think also that the masterworkers in each craft are more honourable and know in a truer sense and are wiser than the manual workers, because they know the causes of the things that are done (we think the manual workers are like certain lifeless things which act indeed, but act without knowing what they do, as fire burns,-but while the lifeless things perform each of their functions by a natural tendency, the labourers perform them through habit); thus we view them as being wiser not in virtue of being able to act, but of having the theory for themselves and knowing the causes. And in general it is a sign of the man who knows and of the man who does not know, that the former can teach, and therefore we think art more truly knowledge than experience is; for artists can teach, and men of mere experience cannot.

Again, we do not regard any of the senses as Wisdom; yet surely these give the most authoritative knowledge of particulars. But they do not tell us the 'why' of anything-e.g. why fire is hot; they only say that it is hot.

SCIENTIFIC METHODOLOGY

Physics is the name Aristotle uses for his science of nature. His physics examines how things move, grow, and change according to their own natures—for example, how and why stones fall, animals jump and crawl around, plants grow, or human beings reason. For Aristotle, in any scientific investigation we have to (1) start from observation and sense perception; (2) study complex things by first studying their simpler parts; and (3) use deductive logic. This scientific method will not merely discover what a thing is made of or describe how a thing acts; it will help us discover a thing's purpose. The question of purpose is important when discussing things in the world as well as when thinking about politics, morality, and, of course, developing a philosophy of education. Aristotle's contention is that we cannot have a philosophy of education without knowing about the principles, causes, and purposes of things.

Four Principles: Material, Formal, Efficient, and Final
To help make sense of things in the world Aristotle describes four principles or causes:

1. Material cause is the matter or stuff from which a thing is made. For example, a table's material cause would be wood.

2. Formal cause is the form or pattern embodied in an individual body. The formal cause is similar to Plato's Forms. We might think of the formal cause like a blueprint within things that makes the organization of matter possible.
3. Efficient cause is what brings the thing into being, the source from which change and motion proceed.
4. Final cause is the end or purpose of the thing.

In his *Politics,* Aristotle stresses the element of purpose or the final cause for human beings. He argues that to know how society could work best we must first discover what it is made up of and what its purpose is. If one wants to make sense of education, one needs to figure out the formal cause of education—one such formal cause might be to foster human essence and our inner potential for good.

Aristotle defines a thing by its form. A thing's matter may consist of wood, stone, water, or whatever else, but the essence of a thing is its form, which is not material. For example, you are more than blood and guts. You have a form, an essence, a soul. It is our souls, not our bodies, which exist as our essences or forms for Aristotle. Plants also have souls, for the soul is synonymous with having life. Without a soul, you would be merely a corpse. The human soul is unlike that of a plant or animal in that it is rational. As we saw with Plato, the rational part of us plays a very important role. Aristotle agrees with Plato in this regard, but he disagrees about how we should act rationally. Aristotle argues that those with rational souls are better suited to be rulers rather than be ruled. He believes that only a few select people are capable of achieving the kind of happiness and rationality that he has in mind, and they do not include females or slaves. A citizen of the state is someone who participates in the activities of the state by holding office and giving judgment. Citizens are exclusively men of the state, because workers, farmers, and women have neither the time nor the appropriate mental development to participate in the administration of justice.

HIERARCHY IN SOCIETY: *POLITICS* IN A NUTSHELL

Aristotle invested a great deal of time and energy trying to understand human nature and the ideal social ordering. It is only as part of this larger social discussion that a philosophy of education might be created. What a proper education consists of can only be discovered after addressing the following questions: What are we? What functions do we have or do we perform? What are our goals and our purposes?

FROM *POLITICS, BOOK II*

When several villages are united in a single complete community, large enough to be nearly or quite self-sufficing, the state comes into existence, originating in the bare needs of life, and continuing in existence for the sake of a good life. And therefore, if the earlier forms of society are natural, so is the state, for it is the end of them, and the nature of a thing is its end. For what each thing is when fully developed, we call its nature, whether we are speaking of a man, a horse, or a family. Besides, the final cause and end of a thing is the best, and to be self-sufficing is the end and the best.

Aristotle sees the state, one's society, as an important form of association with different parts. Relying on his scientific methodology, he studies the state by first looking at its components:

1. Household: the association of man, woman, and slave established for the satisfaction of daily needs.
2. Village: the association of a number of households for the satisfaction of something beyond daily needs.
3. State: the association of several villages that makes leisure and self-sufficiency possible, as well as creates the possibility of a good life for its members.

Through his examination, Aristotle concluded several interesting things about the nature of society and those within it:

1. Society, one's polis, is a thing of nature. Societies are not merely collections of people grouped together in haphazard or purely artificial configurations. Rather, societies naturally arise.
2. Humans are political animals by nature. It is our born disposition to be social and political. It is not a choice we make when we are born.
3. One's society has priority over the individual. Importance is given to both individuals and the larger group, but emphasizes the importance of the larger body or association.
4. Humans may only achieve their full potential (virtue) as members of a society. If we are to grow as individuals we must do so as social beings.

Because we are social creatures, we must look to nature, our natural social selves, in order to make sense of our purposes. When we do, we will see that our purpose is to achieve virtuous character, as individuals, and as a society. Aristotle's philosophy of education encompasses all of these elements.

By observing nature, we see that there is a natural order of ruling and ruled that exists for the sake of both. The naturally ruling has superior reason. The naturally ruled obey the ruling. This hierarchy is evident throughout nature, and it is to the advantage of all that this basic hierarchy exists. To deny it would invite disaster and disharmony. According to Aristotle, the soul has two parts: one that rules (reason) and one that is ruled. Nature determines in which order these parts come. Slaves, for example, exist by nature and also lack the ability to reason. Observing that slaves were consistently strong and large, Aristotle concludes that a slave's purpose is to be used as an instrument. Women invariably deserve respect and honour, but they remain bound by their natures to be dependent upon men. Because women are naturally designed to serve the family as good wives and mothers, and to remain out of the public sphere, it would be unnatural and unfair to expect more of them. In terms of education, not everyone should be expected to receive the same or achieve the same.

The Best Political System and the Golden Mean

Reflective of his image of the ideal individual, Aristotle's ideal political system is practical and moderate. The ideal society will be ruled by a practical constitution that is middle class. The middle class represents moderation as it constitutes a mean between the rich and the poor. Because the middle class consists of property owners it wants the state to run well (it has a stake in things) and it is inclined to be moderate in its decisions (no radical Platonic ideas). By living a moderate life between extremes, the middle class is more likely to follow reason than emotional or selfish extremes. Neither oligarchy (ruled by a few rich elites) nor democracy (ruled by all) is ideal, for Aristotle, as too much power in one group will generate discontent and dissension. Civil war will follow between the powerful and the powerless; therefore we need a polity of the middle class.

The question of moderation is part of Aristotle's famous argument known as the mean between extremes or the golden mean. His claim is simple: aim to live in such a way that you avoid deficiency (too little) and excess (too much). Thus, if you act virtuously in terms of courage, you are neither too confident, and therefore rash, nor too insecure, and therefore cowardly. If you are modest, you are neither shameless (too little shame) nor easily embarrassed (too much shame). However, finding the right balance in practice is far from simple. We should think of the golden mean as a helpful device to remind us that we should try to live better, rather than as a specific course of action to follow—it is not a law telling us what to do in specific circumstances. Knowing how to act appropriately is often not possible until one is faced with a situation and is then able to weigh the pros and cons. Aristotle does not presume to know exactly how each of us should act at those times, only that we should strive to find the best of all possible options. In this sense, a philosophy of education would not prescribe specific acts in life, but prepare us to judge wisely for ourselves.

VIRTUE, ETHICS, AND HAPPINESS

Aristotle argues that the ultimate reason for education is happiness. Happiness can only be attained through virtuousness, and only after one has been trained, nurtured, and educated in a specific way of living. Happiness is more than having a great job, lots of money, or physical pleasure. Whatever happiness is it requires virtue and virtue is very hard to develop. Simply put, virtues are the qualities of a thing that we regard as a good example of something. In Plato's account, virtue consists mainly as a kind of knowledge. In Aristotle's account, virtue is the good state of the soul, like health is to the body. Virtue is a disposition to perform certain actions and to feel certain feelings. Virtuous living means having knowledge of things and an ability to apply knowledge appropriately. Ultimately, virtue means having practical wisdom or prudence.

HEDONISM

Hedonism is the view that the primary good in life is maximizing pleasure and minimizing pain. Today, the most visible philosophy that incorporates hedonism is utilitarianism. Jeremy Bentham and John Stuart Mill argue in favour of utilitarianism, although they do so very differently. However, while their views conflict, both agree with the basic goal of utilitarianism, which is to maximize the most amount of happiness for the greatest number of people. The most popular criticism of this approach is that minorities must suffer in order for the majority to gain, thereby creating a proverbial steamroller flattening the few for the purpose of pursuing the happiness of the greater number.

Aristotle offers something of a common-sense virtue ethics, as well as criteria that actions should meet in order to be virtuous. A virtuous act is done knowingly, not in ignorance, and not motivated by selfishness. Though we seek out what is good in the same way that plants and animals do, according to Aristotle's definition, animals cannot know happiness. Pleasurable actions, and behaviour that results in pleasure, do not warrant happiness. Aristotle's requirement of virtue calls our attention to what we do, as well as how and why we do it. The goal of a moral action must be beyond one's own good—we must do the right thing for the sake of what is noble, not the immediate reward. Additionally, to be virtuous one must act in a steady manner, driven by an unchangeable character, and not flippant or impulsive. Ethics is largely a matter of one's character in action in the world. It is no surprise that Aristotle believes that education must be largely about developing one's character, and therefore their virtue.

To help clarify the notion of virtue, it is helpful to look at Aristotle's distinction between moral and intellectual virtues. **Moral virtue** refers to excellence of character, and it is connected to the desiring or passionate part of our souls. It comes into existence primarily through habit. The more we routinely do something the more it will become a part of our character. The process of habitualization (habit) is the repeated action of making something become second nature even though we are forcing ourselves. For Aristotle, virtue is more than knowledge and overcoming ignorance; it is about our daily action. Because we have the freedom to choose what we know is not right, we must develop a habit of making virtuous choices. Aristotle realizes that habit-forming is difficult and may feel unnatural, but the intentional effort to do good should make life more manageable—it is too easy to allow our passion-prone natures to overwhelm reason. Encouraging the good through habit helps to combat more basic instincts that might corrupt our character, and thus, a philosophy of education must teach students how to *force themselves* to be good.

Intellectual virtue refers to the excellence of our reason. It is connected to the rational part of our souls. Intellectual virtues are excellences of our understanding. They are developed though habit, like moral virtues, but also through education. Intellectual virtues are not manifest through the mean or middle-way, but the actualization of a natural disposition. As we have heard, some people are born to be more rational than others, and therefore with greater potential for greater happiness. These people should be educated in ways best suited to their capacity.

Virtue is a way of living well by habit, education, and practice. We all have a natural inclination to fulfill our purpose and our purpose is to be happy. Happiness requires the ability to make prudent choices. Such virtuous acts are possible when we understand the world well enough to make smart choices. Happiness is both an emotional and intellectual harmony; it is finding the mean between extremes.

There is an unbreakable connection between happiness and philosophical thought. Like many other philosophers, Aristotle holds the highest form of happiness to be contemplation. Philosophical reflection fulfills the most aspects of happiness for it is continuous, pleasant, self-sufficient, and loved for its own sake. The best life is one in which one realizes or actualizes the best possible version of oneself. The best possible version of oneself is the most rational self. The most rational among us is also the happiest among us.

CONSIDER:

What is virtue? How important is it in contemporary society?
Do you agree with Aristotle about the connections between virtuousness and happiness? Do you think being rational is synonymous with being happy?
Do you think animals are capable of experiencing happiness?

Friendship in the Nicomachean Ethics

Defining love and friendship is no easy task, and yet it is often the case that both are implicated in a discussion of happiness. Aristotle argues that friendship requires at least three things: (1) equality; (2) goodwill; and (3) self-love.

Equality is often a politically charged term. Aristotle is not drawing our attention to issues of human rights; he is arguing that friendship differs depending on the relationship. In the same way, duties associated with love also change depending on the relationships—for example, parent-child, husband-wife, and boss-employee. There is sure to be some kind of inequality among friends; however, if there is too much, too great a disproportionality, true friendship will be impossible. One might have a relationship of sorts with those who are not approximately equal, but such cannot be a genuine friendship.

More controversially, Aristotle claims that while equal character—not just similar interests or commonality—is necessary for friendship, the better person should be loved more. For instance, parents deserve more love from children than the children deserve from parents. Total equality is unlikely, so we should be prepared to love people differently depending on who they are and what kind of relationship we have with them, as well as factoring in their intrinsic worth.

Friendship requires goodwill insomuch as one wishes another wellness and happiness. We do not generally stay friends with those who harm us—although actions of goodwill are somewhat unclear, it is presumed those of good character will know what they are.

Finally, Aristotle argues that self-love is important—the virtuous person should love himself. This does not mean one loves him or herself above all others, but that one is in agreement with oneself—for example, there are no conflicting desires. For while the bad person will make things worse for himself by allowing the internal conflict to continue, the good person who loves himself will foster virtue. Those who abuse themselves do not have a healthy self-love and do not live wisely.

We might add one more condition that seems almost too obvious to mention. Friendship requires other people. It would seem that the more virtuous, good, and self-loving one is the less he or she needs to be around others. The virtuous simply do not need things (pleasure, help, or encouragement) from friends. Aristotle believes that we need friends to be fully happy. Again, we are happy when we are acting virtuously and as nature designed each of us to act. Part of virtue is caring for others and being mindful of their virtue, needs, and happiness. If we want to be really happy, to flourish to the best possible degree, we must do so among other political animals. However, while we may need friends we do not need all kinds of friendships. For instance, if friendship is based primarily on pleasure or if it is a utility friendship these are clearly imperfect relationships, according to Aristotle. In pleasure-friendship and utility-friendship we do not love the person but what he or she offers and does for us. These are short-lived and imperfect friendships because people and needs change. Real friendship begins when one genuinely wishes the other person well for his or own sake, rather than because of what one may get from the situation. One is able to wish the others well because he is happy and virtuous. He does not need something from the other person except the other person with whom to practice acts of virtue—a relationship based on virtue of character shared between people and the opportunity to exercise one's own virtues. In short, two good people are able to be friends precisely because they do not need pleasure or utility from one another. Instead, they treat one another as opportunities to flourish because that is what good people do, grow in virtue together. Friendship is not a means to an end. It is an end in itself.

CONSIDER:

What is friendship to you? Do you agree with Aristotle? Are modern forms of online networking congruent to Aristotle's ideals of friendship?

Is it possible to truly be friends with our pets, small children, or those who harm us?

Do you think that some people should be loved more than others?

How would you feel about paying tuition to a university that required you to take character development courses in addition to your courses?

ARISTOTLE'S PHILOSOPHY OF EDUCATION

Children should be taught to follow social norms and laws as this kind of education creates youth capable of becoming good civic participants. Aristotle did not think it was wise to give rigorous instruction to students up to the age of five, for such an education might be a stumbling block. Like Plato, Aristotle argues that the environment of the young should be carefully monitored and controlled. Aristotle argues that there are four main areas or subjects that students should learn from the ages of 7 to 21: reading and writing, gymnastics, drawing, and music. Between Aristotle and Plato there seems to be a fair bit of agreement regarding the basics of sound curriculum plans. However, following rules and social norms is not enough for attaining happiness. Children are expected to learn moral virtues, and only later, when they are able, are they expected to learn intellectual virtues. Physical education is important to Aristotle (and to the Greeks in general), but physical training should not be done while ignoring the training of the mind. A healthy balance between educating the mind and also the body is essential.

Aristotle claims that we all naturally start out aiming toward the good life of happiness and human flourishing. However, some of us go astray early on and need to be encouraged to return to the correct path. Aristotle argues that the individual's education is for the sake of society and we may only achieve happiness as social participants. That is to say, the personal good is important, but so too is the good of the greater society. The best city is the one best able to provide an opportunity and environment for real happiness and the exercise of virtue. Having been educated into certain habits, and then educated into intellectual virtues, it is then possible to be happy. The educated will be able to choose among the best alternatives. They will be able to act rationally, prudently, and moderately without succumbing to vices. When we have educated ourselves as a society, hopefully we will have the ideal state, one filled with the best of human potential.

CR

DISCUSSION QUESTIONS
AND LEARNING ACTIVITIES

1. Does contemporary society prioritize education as something that should be done for the sake of the greater good?
2. Should men and women always and in all ways be treated equally? Is there a case to be made that some of us should be educated differently depending on our natures or character?
3. What are your thoughts on the idea that things by nature have an inherent purpose or goal? Do you think this true for human beings, animals, or plants?
4. Do you think there is a fundamental difference between what a thing is (essence) and what it is made of?
5. Try the following thought experiment: Imagine an ideal society in which all of its members are happy. Describe the sorts of things people do on a daily basis.
   a) Is this a world of leisure, work, or contemplation?
   b) How did your imagined society get to a point of genuine happiness and flourishing? What roll did science and technology play?
   c) What is the dispersal of wealth in your imagined society? Is there monetary wealth, property, physical pleasures, or luxury?
   d) Have sickness and disease been eradicated?

Chapter 3

Locke

Learn through experience and our own perspectives ☞

It is one thing to show a man that he is in error, and another to put him in possession of the truth.
　　　　　　　—Locke, *An Essay Concerning Human Understanding*

I grant that good and evil, reward and punishment, are the only motives to a rational creature: these are the spur and reins whereby all mankind are set on work, and guided, and therefore they are to be made use of to children too.
　　　　　　　—Locke, *Some Thoughts Concerning Education*

INTRODUCTION

This chapter identifies the importance of John Locke's theory of knowledge and mind for a philosophy of education, explores the mechanistic quality of his philosophy, and examines the merit of his notion of *tabula rasa* (blank slate). This chapter will also consider Locke's contribution to the famous debate over whether nature or nurture is the main driver of human development.

John Locke (1632–1704), sometimes called the Father of Liberalism, was a social and political philosopher, as well as a trained medical doctor, and easily one of the most important of early modern thinkers. His contributions to the philosophy of education are less known, though nonetheless important. Widely regarded to be the founder of empiricism (though some credit this

Nuture plays larger role in ed than nature

to Thomas Hobbes, 1588–1679), he put forward an incredibly influential approach to questions of experience and knowledge. Locke's theory of knowledge, discussed in his most famous work, *An Essay Concerning Human Understanding* (1690), dominated for almost 100 years. *Some Thoughts Concerning Education* (1693) also proved very popular, influencing major education theorists such as Jean-Jacques Rousseau.

The connections between Locke's development of empiricism as a theory of knowledge and his views on education are not as obvious as one might hope. Part of the problem is that scholars often treat his philosophy of knowledge and his philosophy of education separately, even though both overlap in important ways. What this means for our investigation is that we must pay close attention to how empiricism is relevant to education, so that we do not miss Locke's foundational ideas in his philosophy of education. For example, one of the most pronounced connections between Locke's empiricism and his philosophy of education is one we have likely all heard before: Is it nature or nurture that creates and determines a person?

Locke believes that nurture is paramount in the educational experience. His epistemological position is that we are empty containers in need of being filled with experience and knowledge. This happens primarily through education. An appropriate education will encourage students to become virtuous, rational, disciplined, and freethinking. Without it, we are but mere blank pages without anything written upon us (or within us). Locke argues that education provides more than knowledge—it provides the elements that make each of us who we are. For Locke, we are by nature open and receptive; therefore, it is nurturing more than a predetermined nature that is responsible for human development.

KNOWLEDGE

Locke's theory of knowledge served both scientific and philosophic progress in important ways. His theory attempts to make sense of how it is that we know the world. Locke argues (contrary to Plato and Descartes) that we do not have innate ideas. We are born without things (without ideas or essences) waiting inside to be released through education. Here is Locke's theory of knowledge in brief:

1. All of our ideas and knowledge are gained through our senses. Knowledge, whether in the form of logic, medicine, psychology, philosophy, botany, or whatever else one might know, is gained through experience.

2. At birth the human mind is a *tabula rasa*—a blank slate, blank tablet, or a blank blackboard.

3. Knowledge is a relationship among our ideas, some of which are simple and some complex. We have a collection of ideas in our minds, and knowledge refers to the agreement or disagreement of those ideas.

4. Ideas include input from the material world, such inputs are primary sensations. Size, motion, number, and mass are properties of objects that act on our senses to produce secondary sensations. Primary sensations are independent of the observer—they belong to the objects—and yet they connect with our minds.

5. Secondary sensations—an object's colour, smell, or sound—are results of primary sensations. We do not relate to secondary sensations as we do to primary ones. Secondary sensations are created within the observer, and are not actually in the world. When one looks at a tree, its primary qualities of size and shape connect with the mind in a manner that its colour does not—its colour is created within the mind. Indeed—this may seem rather odd—Locke maintains that the colour of the tree does not belong to the tree itself; rather, it is an idea in the mind of the observer.

Locke strongly opposes the rationalists who claim that we may know about and experience the world without reliance on the senses. On the contrary, we must experience the world if we are to know it. We know the world because it inscribes upon our blank slates as we experience it through our senses. Strangely, Locke argues that knowledge is not *of the world* but *of our ideas of the world*—that is, knowledge is not a direct connection with the world (with the exception, perhaps, of primary sensations) but an association among ideas in our minds. Knowledge arises because sensations form complex ideas in our minds. It is unclear in Locke's theory why certain ideas are attracted to one another in order to form more complex ideas; even so, his contention is that they do exactly that. The other source of ideas is reflection. This is the ability of the mind to reflect on its own activities. These two sources provide the building blocks of all knowledge and understanding.

For rationalists, reason is the source and justification of knowledge. Whereas Locke argues that truth is sensory, the rationalists argue that truth is deductive and intellectual—it is, at least in large part, independent of experience. Plato and Aristotle are often categorized as rationalists from antiquity, whereas René Descartes (1596–1650), Gottfried Leibniz (1646–1716), and Immanuel Kant (1724-1804) are examples of modern rationalists. It is important to note that while most rationalists and empiricists, such as Locke, may seem to disagree, these two views are not necessarily mutually exclusive. One may be both a rationalist and empiricist without contradiction.

According to Locke, the mind abstracts, generalizes, and combines ideas. The propositions we develop through these activities—the truths we propose—are reliable in a meaningful way, and yet they are only probable in degrees of certainty. Locke argues that we can never be certain because knowledge is particular rather than universal. His empiricism cannot guarantee that our representations of the world are true. This is a radical notion to argue, as many prominent philosophers (for instance, Plato and Aristotle) believe that genuine knowledge must be universal and certain—Locke's account of knowledge is that it seems to be particular and probable, limited in scope and availability. If all ideas arise from experience, it follows that our knowledge must be limited to what we individually encounter.

FROM *AN ESSAY CONCERNING HUMAN UNDER-STANDING* (BOOK 1, CHAPTER 1, SECTION 6)

To say a notion is imprinted on the mind, and yet at the same time to say, that the mind is ignorant of it, and never yet took notice of it, is to make this impression nothing. No proposition can be said to be in the mind which it never yet knew, which it was never yet conscious of. For if any one may, then, by the same reason, all propositions that are true, and the mind is capable ever of assenting to, may be said to be in the mind, and to be imprinted: since, if any one can be said to be in the mind, which it never yet knew, it must be only because it is capable of knowing it; and so the mind is of all truths it ever shall know.

CONSIDER:

Does Locke's account of empirical knowledge seem reliable or
    dangerous? How much can we rely on our senses?
Is the real world something we cannot definitively know?
How does Locke's approach affect science and religion?

Minds and Machines

Locke believes that what we become is mostly a result of our experiences with the world. We are blank slates upon which nature and society write. Education is paramount—it may be used to create any kind of person, whether evil, good, adaptable, or ineffectual. It would be too reductionist, too simplistic, to claim that we are simply the product of our education alone, and yet this is basically the case. In another sense, we become ourselves by learning how to make our own choices. Personal decision-making, rational deliberation, and critical thinking are all very important themes for Locke. Locke argues that education should foster the development of free *machines looking for inputs (experiences)*

and rational minds. This development is directly related to how we are shaped and conditioned by our contexts.

At heart, Locke's view is mechanistic. We are neutral mechanisms at birth, like machines capable of many things, depending on our input. Nature does not predetermine who we are or who we will become, with the exception of a few remarkable people who seem to be naturally gifted. It is interesting to note Locke's acceptance that we have innate talents and interests at birth—things parents would do well to observe and encourage—such talents and interests are not content or knowledge. All knowledge to be written upon us comes through experience, such as education. The question of education and learning seems to largely be a matter of competent programming.

→ learn from exp.

A BRIEF HISTORY OF CLASSICAL EMPIRICISM

Empiricists believe that knowledge is derived from experience. They commonly tackle a similar set of major questions:

- How does the mind work?
- How might we connect knowledge and experience?
- How do our concepts of things relate to things as they actually are in the world?

The famous empiricist conundrum is basically this: *all that we can know are our ideas about things.* This claim leads to a big problem: if our concepts of things are not really of the things themselves then we cannot really know things!

If knowledge is limited to experience, then we can only know our *ideas about things*, and the material universe might suddenly be out of reach.

The classical empiricists include John Locke, George Berkley, and David Hume. All three wrestled with the question of how it is that experience might be both the source of and constraint on knowledge. One of Locke's most famous quotes is also one of his most informative: *Nothing is in the mind that was not first in the senses.* His philosophy of knowledge makes three bold claims:

1. What we perceive and the ideas we have come through our senses and reflection, rather than directly to us as the things themselves.
2. Physical objects cause our perceptions, but our ideas and sensations are what we know—we cannot be sure that our ideas match the world.
3. Experience cannot tell us many important things. We simply cannot know with certainty as we are limited by our experience of the world.

Locke's basic reasoning serves as the foundation to other empiricists, each of whom works out even more radical consequences.

George Berkley

George Berkley (1685–1753), an Anglican bishop, is well known for his *Treatise Concerning the Principles of Human Knowledge* (1710). Berkley argues that Locke fails to realize just how limited we are if we accept empiricism. One of Berkley's more controversial claims is his denial of the existence of matter. He argues that there are only ideas and the minds that hold them. While materialists believe everything in the universe is made of matter (even souls), Berkley argues that we have no direct experience of matter (mind-independent material). Berkley is often described as an idealist. **Idealism** argues that reality is in some way a production of the mind.

Berkley argues that experiences are only the sensory properties of the thing we are experiencing, not the thing itself. In other words, we only have ideas about what we are experiencing; we do not actually know the thing itself. If we *actually* perceived matter, we would know the material object itself—in other words, the fruit. We would know the thing that has the properties, the fruit, not just its properties: the sensory things we perceive, taste, smell, and so on. Again, the fruit causes us to have ideas, but we do not really know the real fruit itself. By contrast, Locke believes that we connect with the real world, the material world, in a meaningful manner (primary sensations). Berkley denies any such connection, for there is no real and material world.

Berkley makes a radical argument: we do not sense matter because there is none. He goes further by arguing that God furnishes our perceptions. It is God who puts ideas into our minds, not a physical reality. Strictly speaking, then, not even the fruit causes us to have ideas. It is God who orchestrates all of our perceptions, both as individuals and as groups.

One of the results of an empiricist stance is the recognition that perhaps we do not need to get behind experience to find reality. If Locke and Berkley are correct that reality is something we cannot know with certainty, then perhaps Plato and those like him are mistaken in the attempt to get behind experience to a more real reality—for instance, a heavenly realm. Instead, as some empiricists have argued, we should look for patterns in our experiences. Once we learn the pattern of how our visual impressions relate to things, we will be able to make inferences about underlying realities. Patterns in experience might not be a lot, but at least they are something by which we may make partial sense of the world. In this way, radically empirical science is not about knowing material things but about understanding patterns in experience.

David Hume

David Hume (1711–1776) is well known for his *A Treatise of Human Nature* (1739), in which he argues for an extreme form of empiricism, making him one of the first radical empiricists. His ideas follow along these lines:

1. Experience provides no real evidence for the existence of anything other than what we currently perceive.
2. Causality is a major concept for our understanding of the world and knowledge itself.
3. We can have no real sensation or ability to observe causation. All we have are our current sensations and experiences, none of which endure or last beyond the moment.
4. Empiricism leads to a radical form of skepticism about knowledge.

For Hume, empiricism means, among other things, that causation is an illusion of sorts, a creation of our minds. Causality is an idea in us—not a fact we experience in the world.

Consider a rock being pushed down a rocky hill: as the rock falls it hits other rocks, sounds are produced and visual impressions are created, and soon there is an avalanche of tumbling rocks. Hume asks if we *actually* see rocks causing other rocks to move; he argues that we cannot perceive the causation or the subsequent movement. It is well accepted today that there exists a transfer of energy from one rock to the other that causes movement. However, Hume would argue that because we do not see this actual transfer of energy, we cannot claim to know the cause of the falling rocks. What we see empirically is a rock moving beside a stationary rock, then two moving rocks beside other stationary rocks, then several moving rocks beside many stationary rocks, and so on. Ultimately, our perception of cause is psychological, not physical. Our perceptions are bound to each separate moment in time. Experience is fleeting—perception of the present is limited in duration, and the future rushes in to fill up the present as the present vanishes into the past. The future is not yet, the past is no more, and the present is but a flash of sensory perception. What we see as causation (rocks moving other rocks) is perceived because the mind joins things together, even though we may not see things being joined literally. Movement is created by the mind making connections between separate events of the present and past.

Hume's radical empiricism jeopardizes the scientific ideas of induction and probability. As a major scientific approach to truth, induction offers probability rather than certainty. And as we saw with Locke, the truth claims of empiricism are probable. Hume, however, argues that we have no rational grounds for assuming probable empirical truth. Our minds may naturally make inductive inferences based on previously experienced patterns, but there is no logical necessity to such inferences. Moreover, Hume rejects all arguments for the existence of God. Whereas Berkley argues that we have ideas because of God, Hume offers no such grounding for knowledge. While most of us accept that the sun will rise tomorrow, Hume argues that there is no empirical reason to support this belief.

CONSEQUENCES OF RADICAL EMPIRICISM

If we are empiricists, all we have as knowledge are sensory perceptions of the present. Unless something exists in front of you right now you cannot empirically claim that it is real, and even then you cannot be certain. Of course, based on patterns of previous experience, it is most likely the case that that which you cannot currently see—your car, family, or pet—still exists. Such things do not typically vanish without cause. Nevertheless, as a logical basis for knowledge our empirical understanding of such realities remains severely limited. There are three main problems with empiricism:

1. **Solipsism**: Solipsism refers to the idea that the only thing that exists for sure is one's own mind. The basic solipsistic problem is that we are stuck in our heads and anything outside the mind is unsure. Many have argued that this is not a necessary consequence of empiricism, but the problem remains important nonetheless.

2. **External World Skepticism**: This problem is related to the first. Classical empiricism leads to radical skepticism. Even if we accept that knowledge is probably true, we still cannot really know much—if anything—about the world beyond our own immediate experiences. The response from many

empiricists to this problem has been rather unsatisfactory. If we accept empiricism in the classical form, there may be no substantial answer to this problem. Indeed, this is a frustrating issue for many radical empiricists.

3. **Inductive Skepticism**: If one of our primary means of knowing is to look for patterns in experience, we need to be relatively confident that the past will resemble the future. Again, the response by many empiricists to this problem has been unsatisfactory. To answer these criticisms directly, empiricism must be rewritten in a fashion unlike Hume's radical version. Since Hume, many have tried different versions of empiricism; nonetheless, many of the newer forms seem to fail in similar fashions.

EDUCATION

Locke has had a major influence on the philosophy of education, especially on views of child development. Much of Locke's discussion of education is geared toward the education of boys who would one day be gentlemen—a particular class of men that, in Locke's day, was more advantaged by status and wealth than most. However, his ideas may serve equally well for children from all classes and sexes. For Locke, men and women may be educated in very similar fashions, except for those ways in which there are "obvious differences" between the sexes. It is not clear exactly what Locke means by this, but whatever he means does not radically alter his philosophy of education or our discussion of it.

According to Locke, a gentleman's education belongs outside the role of government-run schools. His position stands in stark contrast to that of Aristotle, who saw education as the responsibility of the state. Instead, a tutor should instruct children at home—under the close supervision and active engagement of the children's parents—and be the primary educator. A tutorial model of education runs a number of obvious risks, such as the possible creation of social isolation for the student. Moreover, a tutored child may be at risk for lacking knowledge of the world or perhaps of being shy around others. Debates regarding the merits and dangers of home schooling remain commonplace today. Locke was well aware of such dangers; however, he argues that the long-term benefits far outweigh such concerns.

Locke believes that children will benefit greatly in the tutorial model as their primary influence will be virtuous adults rather than undisciplined and irrational children. Locke expects children to become fully functioning and well equipped social creatures—the education that comes from being a part of the youthful herd is far less useful than that which comes from the virtuous example of adults. Following the example of adults is important because Locke argues that a basic aim of education is to train the young to one day serve society, to be a helpful part of the larger world.

Locke was aware that many children from working classes, or those from poor families, must by necessity receive their education from teachers in schools. He was highly skeptical of the school system of his day, though he did recognize the practical reality that many people lack the funds and opportunities needed to receive the best education.

Locke avoids the extreme position of claiming that we are all strictly passive agents completely determined by our environments, as if we had no free will. We are not simply sponges waiting to absorb information—our minds are active, constantly working to seek out new knowledge and challenging ideas. However, we are sponge-like in that we are essentially reactionary—that is, our minds remain at rest until we are affected by experience and our senses receive input from the world. If we are blank slates that know through our senses, then we must rely on external stimuli to shape us, to provide us with ideas.

Education as Liberty

Education has been used by some as a tool for enforcing obedience to governments and other authorities that flourish because of our blind conformity. There are a great many dangers associated with who it is that controls education. Locke argues that genuine education is possible because we all naturally aim toward liberty. Education should respond to our natural inclination to be autonomous and free. Too much authority or demand for conformity will stunt our development. Curiosity and liberty guide every child; we see this in their constant questioning of the world around themselves. We should encourage, but never force, these activities. Liberty, in part, means having a sense of independence. Any activity may become a burden to a child if forced upon them.

One of the unique arguments in Locke is that we should avoid relying on tradition or social convention in the education of our children. We must rely on our own reasoning. We may be afraid of trying new things or adapting to the needs of our children, but we must do so if we are to educate them appropriately. Forcing children to learn in certain ways because such ways are traditional may be disastrous. Careful parents and tutors must be constantly vigilant in discerning new ways of encouraging the individual capacities and traits of children. One form of education does not fit all. Relying on one form of education restricts liberty as well as the best development of each unique individual.

Education as Play

Locke goes so far as to recommend that education be seen as a form of play to children. Indeed, an educator capable of making learning enjoyable is a highly skilled one. If we make education unnecessarily difficult, no one will want to do it. Parents should observe their children to discern which activities they enjoy more, as children will have different aptitudes that should be encouraged if they are going to enjoy education.

Plato saw education as difficult, long, and even painful. Locke argues that we need to connect our natural desire for enjoyment with education. Obviously, not all education may be about pure entertainment, yet Locke's basic argument remains. We should encourage natural desires of curiosity and play rather than overemphasizing education as inherently difficult and painful.

One of the peculiar oddities in Locke's approach to education is his belief that we should teach dancing to children as soon as they are capable. Although Locke is unclear precisely why, he thinks that learning to dance will foster "manly" thinking. Also, perhaps more obviously, there is benefit in the social aspects and mechanical development of learning how to dance. Through dance one learns how to be graceful, to move one's body in a refined manner, as well as learning how to properly conduct oneself as a social creature. Learning to dance is an example of Locke's mind-body integration. It is insufficient to develop the mind alone. The body must be developed as well. Moreover, the development of one will help the development of the other, for Locke believes that we ought to educate the whole self.

A Sound Mind, A Sound Body

Parents must be attentive to the physical health of their children. Children have basic physical needs that should be addressed if we wish them to do well. This may seem like an obvious point, and yet for many philosophers from Plato onward there is less and less attention given to nurturing the body for the sake of education. Locke emphasizes that without health of the body, health of the mind is far more difficult to attain. Plato, by contrast, represents the life of Socrates as one in which freedom from the body, its needs and passions, meant being free in mind—a most worthy goal.

Authority, Manners, and Discipline

According to Locke, the best way to motivate children is for parents to appeal to a child's desire to be valued and esteemed in the eyes of others. Resorting to physical punishment or physical pleasure will encourage the wrong values and result in sensational or physical passions instead of intellectual dispositions. If we are not careful, we may end up encouraging slavish children through rewarding or disciplining them inappropriately—in other words, by beating them into conformity or holding them responsible through fear and intimidation.

Instead of strict obedience to rules, children are to be motivated by desires to avoid disgrace and to be valued for their efforts. Esteem and respect are far better than fear and intimidation. Of course, such efforts to earn the esteem of parents through rational choices and responsible actions, especially in the early years, will be imperfect and awkward. Children learn how to become good through imitating the good seen in others. They learn by example, so parents should provide the best examples possible.

Locke believes that there should be a clear sense of parental authority early on in the lives of children. At the core of his philosophy of education, Locke believes that children want to be rational and known for their ability to be reasonable—parents are not enforcing an attitude that is essentially alien to children; they are encouraging growth in a natural disposition.

Age Appropriateness and the Role of Parents

Locke recognizes that children develop at different rates. Being silly or foolish is an age-appropriate behaviour, rather than a sign of inherent fault, and it would be a mistake to drive out such immature actions through fear and punishment. We should accept such behaviour and do our best to inspire the young to grow through our own good example. They are not yet adults, so we should avoid lofty expectations that would only frustrate them. However, it would also be a mistake to set our expectations too low. Indeed, Locke has fairly ambitious goals for the development of the young and implores parents to treat children as rational agents worth respect.

It often seems that many parents in contemporary society treat their children with a high degree of indulgence. A child or toddler is rarely required or expected to do much. As the parent of a toddler, we expect very little from him and cater to his every need—there is no point in our being strict authoritarians, as the child is responsible for very little. Later, as children develop in their capabilities and responsibilities, parents tend to become more strict or authoritative. A stronger authority is necessary to "keep the child in line," so to speak. Moreover, a stronger, less indulgent position is widely believed to be in the interests of the child's overall development. Some modern parents act more like peers with their children and toddlers but more like police with their teenagers—Locke believes that this form of treatment will keep children from becoming disciplined. He advocates for reversing the order of authority. Young children are to be treated with a high degree of authority and control and, hopefully sooner rather than later, eventually given more freedom to make their own choices. Parents should aim to become more friend-like than authoritarian as their children age. The almost cliché actions of rebellious teenagers might be an indication that those children either did not have a strong example of authority in early childhood or perhaps that parental authority is currently overbearing. Whatever the case may be, Locke believes that children should have respect or awe for their parents, not fear or animosity. The job of parents is not to create slavish and broken children, capable of following every command; rather, the goal is rational and moral individuals able to be their own sources of will and good conduct. The more moral, the more rational a person, the more respect he or she deserves in Locke's account.

Virtue and Reason, Habit and Discipline

Two of Locke's central goals in education are to encourage virtue and reason—he wants children to become disciplined critical thinkers. Moreover, Locke seems to think children are capable of becoming adults quickly, at least by today's standards. For Locke, becoming virtuous primarily means being capable of two things: (1) self-denial, and (2) rationality. Like Aristotle in this regard, Locke regards habit formation as key to virtue development. However, it is important that we be careful about merely learning the habits of those around us for the sake of mimicking others. Locke wants the virtuous and rational person to challenge authority, especially the authority of custom. If children are able to embrace a rational disposition through habit, this will enable them to become freethinking. Yet, habit is only the beginning. Children should grow to be autonomous freethinkers. Virtue comes to us by being embraced through disciplined habit, habit based in large part on our observation of good people. The goal is to make decisions without succumbing to one's passions, one's desires, or the social authorities.

FROM *TWO TREATISES ON GOVERNMENT* (CHAPTER 9)

If man in the state of Nature be so free as has been said, if he be absolute lord of his own person and possessions, equal to the greatest and subject to nobody, why will he part with his freedom, this empire, and subject himself to the dominion and control of any other power? To which it is obvious to answer, that though in the state of Nature he hath such a right, yet the enjoyment of it is very uncertain and constantly exposed to the invasion of others; for all being kings as much as he, every man his equal, and the greater part no strict observers of equity and justice, the enjoyment of the property he has in this state is very unsafe, very insecure. This makes him willing to quit this condition which, however free, is full of fears and continual dangers; and it is not without reason that he seeks out and is willing to join in society with others who are already united, or have a mind to unite for the mutual preservation of their lives, liberties and estates, which I call by the general name—property.

CONSIDER:

Do you agree with either Locke or Plato on the relationship between education and the body?

Do children need to be ruled by fear in order to develop the best kind of learning skills and abilities? Should we have strict rules for children to follow, and when these rules are violated, should we enact strict authoritative punishments?

Do children need to be more or less left to govern themselves and develop at their own pace without fear of punishment?

Should we expect discipline to be naturally occurring from within as the child develops or as something imposed from outside until the child may learn to harness it within?

> How well have your teachers and educational institutions appealed to your sense of wanting to be esteemed and respected?
>
> What are your thoughts on the basic relationship between parent and child as described by Locke?

THE STAGES OF EARLY CHILDHOOD DEVELOPMENT

Locke argues that several important subjects are crucial to the early development of children, and it is the knowledge gained from these subjects that will continually serve them in our daily lives:

1. Reading: If one is capable of talking, Locke believes that one should learn how to read. Learning how to talk is an important feature of education; however, learning how to read at one or two years of age is somewhat more difficult.
2. Memory: Memory should be trained in the young. Good memory rarely happens by accident and having a strong ability to memorize will support Locke's other educational goals.
3. Writing: Once able to read proficiently, the child (perhaps aged five to seven) should be taught how to write. Today, we might add typing as an important element of writing.
4. Language: A child who is capable of speaking English (presumably the native tongue) should be taught a second language, such as French. Locke differs from many philosophers in that he thinks the second language should be a contemporary language that may be of use to the child. Learning a dead language such as Latin may be of some value, especially in academic circles, but priority should be given to the practicality of living languages. Today, we might add Mandarin, Spanish, Hindi, and Arabic as some of the most widely spoken languages in the world.
5. Other subjects: Locke believes that we should also learn arithmetic, geography, history, and geometry. These are important

to him because they are practical subjects essential to operating effectively in the world. These subjects are uncontroversial by today's standards.

It is interesting to note that both art and science are noticeably absent from Locke's curriculum. Drawing may be of some use, he accepts, but poetry and music are of little benefit. His reasoning for the exclusion of science is clearer than for his exclusion of art. The sciences of Locke's time were incredibly different from what we know as science today. Science had not yet "come into its own," so to speak, such that it would be an obvious choice for education. Locke, a trained medical doctor, lacked enthusiasm for the scientific thinking of his time. If he were alive today, Locke would probably have a different view regarding the importance of science study, especially for those sciences that remain driven by basic empiricist beliefs.

CONSIDER:

In an age of digital recording, communication, and online search engines, is the fostering of greater memory something we prioritize?

Is the next generation of learners at risk of losing something important if they are no longer expected to master handwriting?

Do you think science and art should be major components of early education?

LOCKE'S PHILOSOPHY OF EDUCATION

Offering several interesting insights into the possible nature and purposes of education, empiricism clearly influences Locke's philosophy of education; consider that Plato offers a clearer connection between his theory of knowledge and his theory of education. Empiricism, as the epistemological position that all knowledge is gained through our senses, challenges many beliefs regarding what it is that we are teaching or learning. Locke seems more optimistic regarding the potential for reason and virtue among the general population than Plato, who reserves the highest reason for philosopher elites. For Plato, we are not so much creating ourselves as we are uncovering our potential. Some of us have much greater potential than others. Locke, by contrast, argues that we are blank slates in need of nurturing, and when this is done correctly, we may become rational and moral.

Locke is outspoken about punishment and the role of play in learning. Plato's philosophy would seem far less harsh and demanding had he considered the need to make education a matter of play instead of emphasizing its challenging nature. These two philosophers sit in clear contrast regarding the motivation behind learning. Perhaps Locke is naive and Plato has a better sense of the reality of education on this point.

Relying on human experience and social context to provide the substance of knowledge, Locke believes our ideas come from experience in this world, not a heavenly and perfect world of Forms. Plato refers to innate knowledge and a superior realm of reality—making his theories far more metaphysical than Locke's.

Nature and reason are in conflict for both Plato and Locke, and reason must win if we are to become moral and rational individuals. Locke and Plato agree that education has the power to liberate. We must learn to challenge ourselves as well as the norms and beliefs that surround each of us if we are to be truly free.

CR

DISCUSSION QUESTIONS
AND LEARNING ACTIVITIES

1. Do you share any of Locke's sympathies with the tutorial model?
2. What do you think are the best ways to encourage human understanding? Do modern experts agree with Locke? Do you agree with Locke?
3. Which side of the nature-nurture debate do you fall on? How much influence does our environment have on who we become?
4. Should human nature be seen as something we must conquer or overcome through reason and discipline?

Chapter 4

Rousseau

ଔ

Man is born free; and everywhere he is in chains.
—Rousseau, *Émile*

INTRODUCTION

In this chapter we will critically evaluate what Rousseau means by **natural man**, and identify possible ways in which society and culture may be frustrating the best forms of education and authentic living. We will continue examining the debate between nature and nurture, as well as explore Rousseau's argument for a distinction between society and the true nature of authentic human life. This chapter will highlight the tension among educational theorists between educating the individual and educating the individual for the sake of society, and situate Rousseau's dual emphasis on "the love of self" and "compassion" within his philosophy of education.

Jean-Jacques Rousseau's (1712–1778) philosophy of education is uniquely personal—that is, his ideas on education reflect his own temperament and character, and are shaped by his personal history more so than the intellectual ideas and philosophies he studied. Born a Swiss citizen, Rousseau had an unusual childhood. His mother died 10 days after his birth leaving his father, a watchmaker, his aunt, and a nanny to raise him. His father had a passion for books, which he passed on to Rousseau. Together they would sometimes read throughout the night—this constituted the closest thing to an education he had. Never attending school throughout his entire life, Rousseau learned to read and write at home outside of a predesigned curriculum and the structures of formal education.

At the age of 13, Rousseau was placed under the care of a minister after his father's business failed and he had to flee due an altercation with a local landowner. Shortly after, Rousseau was made an apprentice to an engraver, and while he enjoyed the work he did not care for the strictness of his employer. Indeed, throughout Rousseau's life he found it difficult to work under authority—regardless of whether that authority was kind or cruel. At 16, he left his apprenticeship and surrogate home, electing to start a new life on his own. He was without any formal education, financial support, or even friends or family upon whom to rely. He spent the next 20 years working random jobs and self-educating. Soon, after striking off on his own, he met Madame de Warens (Françoise-Louise de Warens). She took Rousseau into her home and became his benefactor. This would be the most important relationship of his life. Madame de Warens gave much to Rousseau. For instance, she gave him access to her library, an important resource for his self-teaching, and she arranged for him to have music lessons. Rousseau would later make his own contributions to music theory, as well as support himself throughout the rest of his life as a music copyist and teacher. Madame de Warens also introduced Rousseau to the life of the aristocracy. The indulgence and decadence of the upper class troubled Rousseau greatly. This corruption would serve as the backdrop to much of his later thought regarding authentic living and politics. Rousseau, a solitary individual unwilling to stay in one place for very long, would return to Madame de Warens time and again over a 10-year period. When he was 20, Rousseau and Madame Warens began an affair. The affair ended when Rousseau learned of her relationship with another man.

After years of struggling on the fringes of various societies, Rousseau committed to living out his philosophical ideals of a primitive or simple life. At the age of 44, he moved into the country, breaking away from his friends and associates. He entered into a common-law relationship with a servant, Thérèse Le Vasseur, whom he had five children with—all of which were abandoned to an orphanage. Rousseau explained his decision simply as something that felt agreeable. He offered little justification except to suggest that his children would be better provided for outside of his care—critics of Rousseau have seized upon this personal choice.

In the country, he wrote three of his most popular and influential works, *Julie, or the New Eloise* (1761), *Émile* (1762), and *The Social Contract* (1762). Rousseau's writings are varied and rich in themes and topics. Consequently, his influence is broad, influencing not only philosophers but also political thinkers, sociologists, psychologists and more. His first major essay, published in 1750, *A Discourse on the Arts and Sciences*, earned him recognition and fame. By the time *Émile* was published, Rousseau had already gained an audience. However, *Émile* attacked conventional ways of thinking, and this upset many, including the government. Rousseau had to flee France to avoid arrest. Returning to Geneva, Rousseau learned that he had upset many intellectuals there as well. At the age of 58 (1770), he returned to France and resumed his work as a music copyist. His remaining years were relatively uneventful, although he showed increasing signs of mental instability.

THE SEARCH FOR AUTHENTICITY AND THE NATURAL MAN

Rousseau's arguments are framed in terms of human experience rather than lofty philosophical abstractions. He does not prize reason above all other human traits, although he accepts that reason may be a form of liberation; he seeks to exalt human feeling and the discovery of a more original self. Rousseau's work is intentionally unique, as he considers himself to be unique not only among other philosophers but among people in general. One of the most important thinkers of the 18th century, Rousseau is known as an outspoken critic of liberalism, especially that of John Locke's, and the **Enlightenment**.

The Enlightenment, or Age of Reason, marks a radical change in human thinking that escapes any simple definition. Beginning in late 17th- and 18th-century Europe, the Enlightenment shifted social and intellectual foundations away from tradition, religion, and superstition, to reason, scientific method, and humanism. At heart, the Enlightenment provided a sense of freedom for the individual to think outside perceived confines of traditional institutions, most obviously the Church.

Romanticism, following the Enlightenment period, beginning in late 18th-century Europe, challenged the ideal of reason by arguing that we ought to give emphasis to emotion instead. For the Romantics, the strict adherence to principles of reason and scientific method overlooked important and essential features of human life including intuition, sentiment, and mystery. In other words, supporters of the Enlightenment had gone too far, having become too reductive in promoting human reason above all our other faculties and abilities.

A predecessor to Romanticism, Rousseau is more emotional than rational, even anti-intellectual in many respects. A sensitive recluse with a great love of nature (except the sea), his unconventional ways of seeing the world put him at odds with the larger Enlightenment ideals of his day, in which reason and science were widely accepted to be the proper means of thinking. Rousseau claimed that both the sciences and arts corrupt humanity. Science encourages moral destruction and the belief in overall cultural progress. People are neither more virtuous nor happy because of science. Moreover, the arts are corrupted and act as platitudes or superficial pleasantries. The arts are ignorant of our real chains and troubles.

Rousseau believes that those who have come before him have failed to look deeply enough at what it means to be human or have a nature. Locke provides an example of philosophical thinking with which Rousseau is deeply troubled, as a number of problems from the empiricist tradition are left unaddressed. Perhaps the most troubling is that if empiricism is true then we are trapped inside our own minds. If this is the case, the search for an authentic self becomes most difficult. Rousseau rejects the basic assumptions of empiricism and refuses to be forced into solipsism. Rousseau disagrees that we are empty containers waiting to be filled. He claims we are born "good" by nature, and the problem we face is the recovery of the goodness that we have lost, or the goodness robbed from us by corrupt societies and cultures.

FROM *THE SOCIAL CONTRACT* (BOOK 1, SECTION 2)

Aristotle was right; but he mistook the effect for the cause. Every man born in slavery is born for slavery—nothing is more certain than that. Slaves lose everything in their chains, even the desire to escape from them: they love their servitude, as Ulysses' comrades loved their brutish condition when the goddess Circe turned them into pigs. So if there are slaves by nature, that's because there have been slaves against nature. Force made the first slaves, and their cowardice kept them as slaves.

In his *Discourse on the Origin and Basis of Inequality Among Men* (1755), Rousseau confronts the question of whether or not humanity may have allowed itself to become corrupted and socially conditioned through the creation of civilization. The fundamentally destructive nature of having a society, any society, cannot be ignored according to Rousseau. While there is much good that has come with the creation of civilization, we must be aware of its dangerous side. His philosophy of education represents an attempt to make sense of what he sees as our destruction. Such an understanding will foster our emancipation, not from society but from its corruption.

To understand better what has gone wrong within civilized cultures, Rousseau proposes a thought experiment in his *Discourse on Inequality*. It is difficult to imagine what humans might have been like before civilization, as even remote tribes around the world are socialized in some respect. Rousseau invites us to envision the primitive human being, granted at the level of conjecture. For some of us, it is tempting to imagine an ideal human being as fully natural and good, living in harmony with nature and others. While Rousseau argues that the natural man is basically good, he realizes that a truly primitive person living beyond the constraints of social norms and laws would be brutish and amoral. Still, according to Rousseau, we may learn something from such a being—such an animal. Two of the most important lessons to be learned from his thought experiment are: (1) we are not by nature social and political creatures; and (2) that we must learn to revive our natural selves as solitary and pre-political. Of course, literally returning to a purely natural uncivilized state is not possible for modern people; Rousseau acknowledges that we must remain in society. Therefore, we are left with some important questions to consider.

CONSIDER:

Has society distorted our natural selves? What does it mean to be a self in society?

What would the self look like before it is socially conditioned?

Do you think human beings are naturally social?

THE GENERAL WILL

In his most famous book, *The Social Contract*, Rousseau discusses how best to organize and structure society—in other words, how legislative power should be controlled and how laws should be created and implemented. His book proved to be highly controversial, inspiring revolutions (especially in France) and political reform. The basic argument Rousseau puts forward is that only the people, as a collective, should have the power to determine the activities of society.

FROM *THE SOCIAL CONTRACT* (BOOK 1, SECTION 7)

The fact is that each individual as a man can have a particular will that doesn't fit, and even conflicts with, the general will that he has as a citizen. His individual self-interest may speak to him quite differently from how the common interest does. He looks at the situation in this way:

'I have an absolute and naturally independent existence; I'm not something that exists only because certain items have come together in an association. So what I am said to 'owe' to the common cause—i.e. to the body politic or sovereign whose existence is in that way dependent on the conduct of its members—is really a gift, a hand-out; if I withhold it, that won't harm anyone else as much as it will benefit me. As for the 'moral person' that constitutes the state, that's not a man but a mere mental construct.'

So he may wish to enjoy the rights of citizenship without being ready to fulfill the duties of a subject; and if that went on for long enough it would destroy the body politic.

To protect the social compact from being a mere empty formula, therefore, it silently includes the undertaking that anyone who refuses to obey the general will is to be compelled to do so by the whole body. This single item in the compact can give power to all the other items. It means nothing less than that each individual will be forced to be free. It's obvious how forcing comes into this, but. . .to be free? Yes, because this is the condition which, by giving each citizen to his country, secures him against all personal dependence, i.e. secures him against being taken by anyone or anything else. This is the key to the working of the political machine; it alone legitimizes civil commitments which would otherwise be absurd, tyrannical, and liable to frightful abuses.

The Social Contract has been frequently misunderstood; mainly because Rousseau's writings are filled with contradictions and reversals in positions. In contrast to other philosophical writings, they are unusually open to differing interpretations. His philosophy has been used to support very different and contradictory ideologies, including democratic and totalitarian positions as well as both conservative and liberal governments.

In *The Social Contract*, Rousseau offers the concept of *the general will* as an important tool for what he believes is the creation of social authenticity. With it, he addresses problems of seemingly perpetual inequality and discontent throughout society. If humans are to be social—and we must be—then it remains to be seen how we might do so while being as natural as possible. Some compromise will need to be made if we are to be both social and authentic creatures.

Today, modern societies have laws to help create equality, including the fair distribution of liberty and resources. For the most part, we might assume such laws are for the benefit of all. Is it possible that some laws enforce the very inequality they are said to safeguard against? Laws are created by people after all, socialized people. In the state of nature, according to Rousseau, inequalities were physical. In modern societies, inequalities are far greater both in quality and quantity, in terms of property, political power, social status, and so on. To answer the question of how we might live together as social beings, governed by laws, while simultaneously minimizing inequality, Rousseau offers his concept of the general will.

Rousseau argues that the foundation of legitimate authority in society (all societies) is the general will. We cannot arrive at justice through one person's will. We need a social contract, one which will form the basis of a common or general will. Kings, queens, prime ministers, and presidents cannot provide the general will that emerges by virtue of a collective morality. This morality is made possible by a social contract through which we will each be protected and given freedom and liberty. In addition to mutual safety (for the contract allows each of us to join with others), we are able to remain individually free. Social contract theorists—such as Locke, the first to introduce the idea of a social contract—have long recognized that social contracts potentially reduce our individual liberties, as one's rights (at least in part) must give way to the rights and needs of the larger group. Rousseau is optimistic that his approach avoids this problem.

Each of us must give ourselves freely to the general, or common, will. This is not an inauthentic act; we are not blindly behaving as a herd. We are obeying ourselves by obeying the general will. When the people become sovereign through the contract, each encounters freedom—no one is dependent on the will of another person, only the totality of the general will. It is all too easy for society to be corrupted and controlled by individuals, but if we give ourselves over to the general will we find a new form of freedom. Such is not a state of nature but a new morality. We lose some of our natural liberty under the new contract, but we gain moral liberty.

Rousseau believes that we are chained by laws and social dependence. These chains may be made legitimate, if we can authenticate instead of breaking them. Each of us, through free consent, should give ourselves to everyone else. No one of us acquires more power over others than is afforded to every individual. Each of us is then a part of the general will. The general will is said to be infallible, as it is above the will of individuals and it is interested in the common good of the people. Laws are expressions of the general will.

Some may reject the general will. They will need to be forced to follow it. Only the selfish would reject the general will, and society is right in working against such selfishness. In effect, this means that some will need to be forced to be free. Absolute liberty, for many, means freedom from constraint and interference, including freedom from law. To be free is to be able to act however one so chooses without fear of authority or punishment. For Rousseau, however, the law (itself a product of the general will) is necessary for genuine and sustainable liberty. Moreover, obeying the general will is obeying a self-imposed law, and this, for Rousseau, offers us moral liberty and freedom.

Traditionally, the idea of liberty and freedom has been seen as belonging to two spheres: public and private. Generally speaking, in the private sphere one is allowed to do whatever one wants, but in the public sphere one has far less liberty, due to various social responsibilities and constraints. Rousseau is drawing these two spheres together such that one's own liberty is realized within the larger sphere of one's existence through the general will. Laws are genuine or legitimate when each of us shares in the creation of them. The generation of a social contract means that we are free from the threat of corrupt political powers and rulers.

FROM *DISCOURSE ON INEQUALITY, PART II*

An unbroken horse erects his mane, paws the ground and starts back impetuously at the sight of the bridle; while one which is properly trained suffers patiently even whip and spur: so savage man will not bend his neck to the yoke to which civilised man submits without a murmur, but prefers the most turbulent state of liberty to the most peaceful slavery. We cannot therefore, from the servility of nations already enslaved, judge of the natural disposition of mankind for or against slavery; we should go by the prodigious efforts of every free people to save itself from oppression. I know that the former are for ever holding forth in praise of the tranquillity they enjoy in their chains, and that they call a state of wretched servitude a state of peace: *miserrimam servitutem pacem appellant.* [Tacitus, Hist. iv. 17. The most wretched slavery they call peace.] But when I observe the latter sacrificing pleasure, peace, wealth, power and life itself to the preservation of that one treasure, which is so disdained by those who have lost it; when I see free-born animals dash their brains out against the bars of their cage, from an innate impatience of captivity; when I behold numbers of naked savages, that despise European pleasures, braving hunger, fire, the sword and death, to preserve nothing but their independence, I feel that it is not for slaves to argue about liberty.

One of the main difficulties with Rousseau's view is that there are significant challenges to its practical limits. The sort of political body he has in mind must necessarily be a small one—nations as large as the United States, Canada, or France would be too large for Rousseau's social contract. And as with any social contract, there is a need for safeguards against harming individuals and minorities. Whenever there is a majority or consensus rule, there is a risk to minority voices that do not agree. In summary, while perpetually concerned with humans living unnaturally within society, Rousseau believes that we may still achieve something like a natural state.

CONSIDER:

Is inequality a fundamental reality of society? Is real equality possible?

How might a common will be given a voice or platform?

What does it mean to be authentic, especially if we cannot expect to flee all social influence and constraint?

SELF AND SOCIETY: TWO FUNDAMENTALS

Rousseau argues for two major elements at the heart of the natural person: love of self and compassion. Rousseau draws a distinction between self-love (*amour-propre*) and the love of self (*amour de soi*). Self-love is how we are seen through the eyes of other social members. Everything we do or think is influenced by other people, conditioned by those around us. Rousseau rejects self-love. He thinks it fosters an inauthentic self, one prone to hostility, contempt, and trivial and petty competition.

By contrast, the love of self refers to self-respect and self-preservation. If we have a love of self, we are more authentic or healthy, according to Rousseau. Natural humans (pre-political) would have had a greater sense of a love of self, he thinks. They would have experienced full equality for such people would have lived without the kinds of competitions and jealousies that we know today. Moreover, men and women would have been equal. It is not until we begin to confine humans to social settings, cultures, marriages, and so on, that we encourage inequality and unhealthy domination. For instance, as agriculture developed, division of labour fostered inequality. With the division of labour and the administration needed to run big business comes a hierarchy of success and failure. Moreover, having property encourages competition and ← greed. Thus, while valuable, the development of agriculture also provided unhealthy competition and an unhealthy sense of pride. Natural humans are not self-destructive or selfish in such ways, according to Rousseau. A natural person lives in a state of healthy self-preservation, not greed, envy, jealousy, or inequality through the domination of others.

While we cannot return to a fully natural and primitive state, perhaps we may at least learn something about ourselves by imagining it. Rousseau believes that we must stop living our lives as others see us, as we are encouraged to be by our societies: *amour de soi* (the love of self) is good. For Rousseau, feeling should be the basis of living. If we are to be authentic, we must live spontaneously in accordance with feeling—we are sensitive creatures, capable of great compassion when freed from the illusions of civilized humanity. Rousseau had witnessed firsthand a lack of compassion to those less fortunate from authorities, intellectuals, and the wealthy—this is a sick form of culture when entire classes of people are less inclined to feel compassion for other classes of people.

Compassion is the beginning of morality for Rousseau. It is developed through an understanding of self and about learning to feel for others what one has felt for oneself. Rousseau believes that we tend to empathize with those who are more pitiful than ourselves. We pity those who are afflicted with problems with which we may also suffer. In other words, we are aware of our shared weaknesses and miseries and this unites us. We are not drawn to happy people, but to those who suffer as we do. According to Rousseau, pity is sweet.

Our natural goodness is our compassion. However, when we become civilized our compassion is pushed aside for calculating reason. Vices rush into the human who has become social—become cultured.

Foundations of Education

Émile

One of the main ways in which Rousseau believes that we
may restore our natural selves is through education. In his
1762 novel—*Émile, or On Education*—Rousseau describes
the role of education for the achievement of human nature.
Thought provoking and engaging, *Émile* is an exceptionally important text for educational theorists. *Émile*
is about trying to allow a child to grow up without being socially
conditioned to fit into a certain stereotypical model, and how we
might allow children to grow up according to their natural inclinations. Nature should educate children, rather than teachers and
books. Both teachers and books are dangerous for they instruct
learners in how society believes they "ought" to learn.

Society and Corruption

As we have partially discussed, Rousseau believes that we are born
good but corrupted by society. Living with other humans inevitably
results in inequality by leading us away from a more simple and natural way of living. Rousseau wants us to return to the primitive state of
humanity. The cultured way of living fosters decadence, viciousness,
and so many other vices. Vices are fostered in children by society, not
nature. In the opening of *Émile*, Rousseau writes:

> Everything is good as it leaves the hands of the Author
> of things [God]; everything degenerates in the hands of
> man.... He turns everything upside down... He wants
> nothing as nature made it, not even man; for him man

must be trained like a school horse; man must be fashionable in keeping with his fancy like a tree in his garden.

As an example of how civilization has changed us, consider Rousseau's argument that the fear of death is not naturally within us. Rousseau argues that it is the fault of those in our environment, especially the highly regarded—priests, philosophers, and doctors—that we fear death. Rousseau's **negative education** is meant to help us overcome this fear. He is hopeful that we may somehow get back in tune with our inner selves, the pre-corrupted versions of ourselves. Through a natural education we may foster better people, people who no longer suppress their natural selves and strive to live authentically. Rousseau believes that we are all equipped with abilities that allow us to develop well and eventually become good civic participants, if such abilities are appropriately encouraged. The natural aim of each individual is to become good, this development is facilitated best by the removal of as many obstacles from the education of the young as possible. We may accept that society is dangerous, but it is also necessary. It is least dangerous when it is least inhibiting and corrupting. The more hands-off it is the better. According to Rousseau, if we let the young develop on their own we will see that they are perfectly adapted to the needs of each stage of life—as illustrated by Rousseau's childhood.

Rousseau's approach may be called organic in so much as human nature is seen as a natural product belonging to a whole being that is active and aimed toward a purpose or goal. This contrasts with Locke's view in which we are more mechanical—machines waiting to be fed with sensations. Rousseau differs a great deal from the empiricists. For Locke, there is no authentic self to which we should be true. We create the authentic self through our experiences of life and through the detailed training of gentlemen.

Negative Education

Negative education is child-centred and is meant to foster autonomous thinking. *Negative* does not mean pessimistic; rather, it represents the child's freedom from constraint and conformity. A well-educated person will have a healthy character, one with a sense of self-worth and morality. Rousseau argues for nature over nurture, and thereby distinguishes himself strongly from the likes of those, such as Locke, who argue for nurture over nature. Education should help children learn how to live naturally, spontaneously, and authentically—it will help guard the child from being corrupted by society. From the beginning of their lives, Rousseau claims, we tend to imprison children, forcing them to conform to social ideals. The natural is subjugated when we prevent children from learning through spontaneous experiences by forcing them to memorize facts and to become knowledgeable in accord with a specific curriculum.

Like Locke, Rousseau has a tutorial mode of education in mind. Both philosophers agree that children are in need of constant supervision. However, Rousseau argues against education in which the teacher is the authority and source of knowledge, as such an education would force people to think in specific ways. A negative education helps us avoid pre-determined ways of thinking. We must learn how to judge and evaluate ideas and actions outside the proverbial box of civilization. Education is about more than teaching facts and knowledge—it is about liberating our natural compassion and spontaneity, as well as helping us see the artificial appetites and desires created by our participation in society.

Rousseau's negative education is less about communicating truths and facts to children and more about safeguarding an open learning environment. There is no specific curriculum that a tutor must follow, no list of subjects to instruct. Instead, the job of the tutor is to protect the natural inclinations (natural goodness) as the child develops through the various stages of early life.

Two Stages of Child Development

Education begins in infancy. There are two general stages in child development, divided into five phases of development. For our purposes, consider the first stage to be from infancy to 12 years and the second stage after 12 years of age. In the first stage, the child is incapable of reason, so the tutor should not try to reason with him. This is the time to develop strong bodies and senses and teach natural consequences to actions though observation. One should avoid teaching about plants and animals from textbooks, and instead experience them firsthand in nature. Learning and understanding should reflect one's growing sense of real needs in life. [Punishment is unnecessary because a child will learn through experiencing the consequences of actions; even morality will be learned in such a way.] In the second stage, the child is expected to begin a period of studying. While the child is mechanical at first, at the second stage he is expected to reason. Curiosity should be encouraged as it will aid the child's ability to solve problems when confronted with trouble or confusion.

We should avoid teaching children what they may learn on their own. Also, we should avoid coddling them or making life too easy. Oddly, Rousseau argued that the only book that should be available is *Robinson Crusoe*. The basic plot describes a lone man on an island making do with his own resources and tools without the aid of others. Rousseau finds the idea of a solitary man congruent to teaching children how to be natural and authentic. Also curious was his insistence that children be educated in rural settings, and only when older should they be allowed to enter cities. He was of the opinion that men and women are inherently different and therefore ought to be taught differently, arguing that men are active and strong and women are passive and weak.

ROUSSEAU'S PHILOSOPHY OF EDUCATION

Locke and Rousseau agree that government-run public schools should be avoided, as children tend to corrupt one another and teachers often follow prescribed curriculums that may not fit the child's needs and interests. They agree that children should be taught by a tutor and that education should begin very early. Additionally, both value freedom in education, allowing children to explore without being overburdened. Education should help toughen the young so that they are prepared for the realities of life. That said, Rousseau overtly disagrees with Locke's view that we should teach children through habit, and rejects Locke's idea that children should be motivated by how they will be perceived by others. Habit and reputation are unnatural, according to Rousseau. Locke's educational theory ends with the goal of gentlemen becoming citizens, while Rousseau's design is focused on the individual becoming less socially intertwined. While reason or rationality are important to both Locke and Rousseau—though for different purposes—Rousseau thinks that reason is something to be avoided in early education until the child is able to think more dynamically.

Rousseau's ideal person is a natural and decent individual; this can be contrasted with Aristotle's loftier ideal of a moderate individual capable of a mean between extremes. Rousseau's Émile is far more individualistic than Aristotle's citizen, who works toward the common good. Self-interest is fundamental to fictional Émile and his education. Though Rousseau accepts that we must all be social, his "political animal" is aimed less toward the good of the whole than is Aristotle's.

Plato's educational goal is to reveal a transcendental good, the ultimate truth; Rousseau believes that emotion and spontaneity are our true guides. Plato's curriculum is geared explicitly toward the development of superior leaders—philosophers kings or queens—and Rousseau has no interest in creating leaders, for such an education would be unnatural and would only foster greater inequality. Whereas Plato is interested in cultivating citizens, Rousseau is interested in our return to our more primitive and animalistic inclinations.

CR

DISCUSSION QUESTIONS
AND LEARNING ACTIVITIES

1. Should we try to overcome our social conditioning in favour of living what Rousseau calls "authentic" lives?
2. Compare and contrast Plato, Aristotle, Locke, and Rousseau's theories of human nature.
3. Rousseau thinks civilization has made us unhappy by fostering an artificial and unhealthy sense of self. Do you agree?
4. If you were to write a fictionalized piece of writing on education, similar to *Émile*, list some of the basic themes you would include.
   a) What would be the basic plot of your story?
   b) What kind of characters, settings, and storylines might you use to depict your philosophy of human development?
   c) What would Rousseau think of your story?

Chapter 5

Dewey

ෆ

The conception of education as a social process and function has no definite meaning until we define the kind of society we have in mind.
—Dewey, *Democracy and Education*

INTRODUCTION

In this chapter we will identify and evaluate the core features of **pragmatism**, and John Dewey's reliance on it for the development of his philosophy of education. We will also explore the parallels and importance of science, democracy, and education, as well as evaluate the merit of Dewey's emphasis on experience and action in his philosophy of education.

John Dewey (1859–1952) was born in Burlington, Vermont. He graduated from the University of Vermont in 1879 and pursued studies at Johns Hopkins University. After receiving his PhD in 1884, Dewey began work in the philosophy department at the University of Michigan, where he remained for 10 years. In 1886, Dewey married Alice Chipman and credits her for the genesis of his interests in social justice and public life. Dewey's position at the University of Chicago saw him gain enough support to begin an experimental school, which he left after controversy arose regarding its administration. In 1904, Dewey joined Columbia University where he remained until his retirement.

One of the most influential education theorists of the 20th century, and easily one of the century's most famous philosophers,

Dewey wrote on many subjects, including psychology, philosophy, and political science. His thinking is systematic, but his writing is often dense and therefore a bit difficult to understand, especially for new readers of philosophy. Some of Dewey's more popular works on education include *The School and Society* (1899), *How We Think* (1910), *Democracy and Education* (1916), and *Experience and Education* (1938).

PRAGMATISM

Pragmatism refers to a particular doctrine of meaning. There are different versions, but the basic doctrine is that the meaning of an idea or term has its meaning insomuch as it guides our conduct. Truth, generally speaking, has a necessary connection with workability or applicability. If a theory or idea works when applied, it may be said to be true. However, just because a theory or idea works today does not mean that it will always work. Thus, just because we may call something true today does not mean that we will always do so. Charles S. Peirce (1839–1914), William James (1842–1910), and John Dewey are the first and most visible pragmatists.

The stereotype of philosophers as ivory-tower thinkers, lacking practicality, drives the pragmatist project. Pragmatism is a response to the idea that the intellectual world has lost its necessary connection to the real world. The philosophical heritage (that comes to us from the likes of Plato, Aristotle, Descartes, Locke, etc.) is fundamentally mistaken, according to pragmatists. If it is to be helpful, it must be mindful of its inherited presumptions regarding the separation of theory and practice. For instance, like Rousseau, the pragmatists are concerned about the traditional notion of the mind as separate from the world. If we maintain the view that knowledge or truth is primarily a matter of correspondence (i.e., the right connection between knowledge claims and the world in itself), then we cannot gain real knowledge. This mistaken view of correspondence relies on a separation of the mind and its ideas from the world. If we accept that there is a separation of the mind from the world, then we are again faced with the problem we encountered with Locke—solipsism.

Pragmatists argue that unless we abandon the basic duality of mind/body or mind/world, we cannot say we know in the best sense. Dewey calls this duality of observer/observed "the spectator theory of knowledge."

Pragmatists claim that the meaning of things must be understood within the context of human actions and social situations—that is, the meanings we each have about ourselves, others, and the world exist in communities and the concrete activities we experience every day. Meaning, indeed knowledge itself, cannot be gained through abstractions or principles alone, as Plato would have us believe. Knowledge, scientific or otherwise, should be seen as something we gain through problem-solving interactions with the world and communications with others. The more we attempt to interact with the world—participate in the world—the more knowledge we gain. A disinterested, detached, or neutral observation of the world cannot provide real knowledge in the sense a pragmatist believes possible. Locke's view, for instance, in which we are blank slates upon which knowledge may be written, is too passive for pragmatists. Real understanding is a product of participation, challenge, experimentation, and interested problem solving. In short, knowledge and understanding are interwoven with human experience.

Knowledge (Truth) and Skepticism

Pragmatists may be characterized as skeptics because certain and absolute knowledge is believed to be a faulty pursuit. While pragmatism has often been a highly naturalistic or scientific way of thinking, this should not be mistaken for a strictly objective enterprise. The primary goal of understanding is actionable truth, workable and applicable truth. This kind of truth is more relevant than that of pure objectivity in the traditional scientific sense.

Pragmatism holds that knowledge comes in degrees of certainty. More generally, knowledge is said to be partial and relative to one's situation. When we pursue knowledge, we endeavour to find that which works for our situation and allows us to succeed, whatever that might mean given the needs of the moment. Knowledge involves more than proven facts or objective data, for real (pragmatic) knowledge is something that allows us to function effectively in the world. True knowledge is true insomuch as it is relevant and applicable to our lives. Any way of thinking that is unrelated to everyday life risks being a waste of time. The fruitfulness of ideas (accepted knowledge) when applied to our lives should be our standard of success. When our experiences are fruitful, revealing, and relevant, we are successful, and our knowledge true. Tomorrow, however, a similar situation may require that we accept different truths in order to be successful.

CONSIDER:

Do humans see the world from a distance, a neutral or detached perspective?

What does it mean for something to be true? Do you think truth is objective or subjective?

How culturally dependent is truth?

Do you see any problems with a pragmatic definition of truth?

Pragmatism argues that truth is whatever will help us achieve goals and make sense of our concrete practical experiences. Truth as abstract principle, textbook fact, or dictate of reason cannot achieve this sense of usefulness. Thus, again, truth is what works and what works is that which helps us achieve the goals and solve the problems we experience in life.

Science and Democracy

In keeping with the scientific tradition, generally speaking, pragmatists are empiricists—to make sense of human knowledge and understanding we must make sense of experience. According to Dewey, early empiricists failed to account for the diversity of actions in experience. Traditional accounts have forced experience into artificial and trivial problems. Real experience, so he believes, is much richer than that described by the likes of Locke and other empiricists. Empiricism (at least Dewey's pragmatist version of it) is believed to be of great practical significance in that it helps us achieve our goals. It may be initially a bit difficult to understand how pragmatism might be scientific, naturalistic, empirical, and yet highly relative and emphatically practical. This is a unique combination of themes that has made pragmatism popular but also difficult to understand. Most traditional accounts hold that true knowledge is something independent of human ideas and actions, something that exists regardless of our beliefs. For Dewey, true knowledge must be understood in experiential terms. Knowledge becomes true through events and processes in life—we make truth. There are no final or absolute truths. Truth is true by contrast to recent events, not by virtue of its unchanging status in reality. This belief makes for a much different empiricism than that of Locke, one in sharp contrast to much of the thinking in the scientific tradition.

Along these lines, we should consider another pragmatist relationship: democracy and science. Science and democracy share many important parallels and similarities. Dewey argues that both democracy and science offer the means for generating greater freedom. If we are to be truly free then we must be democratic and this democratic freedom must possess specific features evident in science—both science and democracy require our active participation and engagement with the world and both require the blending of theory and practice. Extremes in political and scientific communities of pure theorizing or pure practice create dangerous misunderstandings and maladaptive thinking. For Dewey, real understanding involves both theoretical and practical aspects. Similarly, democracy involves the inclusion of voices and opinions, just as healthy scientific practice involves observations and ideas, from as many people as possible.

Dewey argues that if we apply some basic scientific methodologies to our social and political context we will be better off as a society because knowledge is best modeled by science. The experimental attitude of science shows how knowledge is gained through our participation in and with reality. The more evidence we gain, the more hypotheses we create and test, the more conversations we include on a matter, and the more experiments we do, the better our knowledge. Science is about going out into the world and engaging with it—we do not gain understanding passively; we gain it by being active agents in the world. If our goal is to understand, we must look to the scientific practice of experimentation as our guide. Such a practice exists within democracy as well; it too progresses by virtue of similar experimental interactions with the world and others. Any inquiry, scientific or otherwise, is successful as long as it gains results; through comparing and contrasting different methods of inquiry, we can learn their respective validity—a process that a democratic environment will encourage.

The Problems of Employing a Scientific Approach

Consider some of the major problems with a scientific approach to understanding:

1. The scientific devices we use and the means in which we employ them will have an effect on the results—the influence of measurement on the measured. Whether it is a microscopic organism illuminated under a microscope or a first-hand observation of buffalo in a field, what a thing is before our scientific measuring may not be the same thing during and after our observations. Light changes microorganisms and the presence of a human on a field will disturb buffalo. To observe the world means we must get involved with it in some manner, which means we often change it in unexpected ways. Our scientific actions change reality and make it much harder to know *as it is*.

2. Science is fallible in its practices and observations. Experimental errors are commonplace and there is constant need to increase accuracy and measurement. If humans are thinking and acting as scientists then errors and mistakes will happen; we can only do our best with the resources we have.

3. The indeterminacy of nature prevents absolute predictions. It is not merely that we lack enough knowledge about reality. Reality itself is intrinsically probabilistic (as exemplified in quantum research) and therefore one cannot easily or simply point to the world and say, "Fact!" The complexity of life is often overwhelming; we must be humble in our claims.

4. Similar to the previous point, the very nature of knowledge means that we may never be sure if we possess facts of a mind-independent reality or if we see things as they really are. The interplay between data in terms of evidence and observation and in terms of theory is continuous—we are continually interpreting evidence. Even when all the evidence supports a given theory or knowledge claim, further data may reveal it to be in error. The recent history of science is full of examples, such as our changing views on light, gravity, particles, and so on.

5. The social character of scientific knowledge is challenging. It was once claimed that all knowledge except scientific knowledge was socially influenced. This is no longer the dominant opinion. We rely on our prior (social) knowledge and (social) experience to make sense of things. This means that our subjectivities (our experiences, memories, beliefs, and assumptions) are necessary for making sense of the world. For example, by merely recording data in the most objective manner possible we are relying on a language and conceptual framework rooted in our own social and historical backgrounds. A *matter of fact* is a social category reflecting a scientific community's paradigm.

The value of this short discussion of science is the realization that scientific understanding, for all of its success, is far more tentative and conditional than many wish to admit. It would seem that the pragmatists have good reason for relying on science, especially its experimental side, while also insisting that absolute or objective knowledge is an illusion.

FROM *DEMOCRACY AND EDUCATION* (CHAPTER 1)

The primary ineluctable facts of the birth and death of each one of the constituent members in a social group determine the necessity of education. On one hand, there is the contrast between the immaturity of the new-born members of the group—its future sole representatives—and the maturity of the adult members who possess the knowledge and customs of the group. On the other hand, there is the necessity that these immature members be not merely physically preserved in adequate numbers, but that they be initiated into the interests, purposes, information, skill, and practices of the mature members: otherwise the group will cease its characteristic life. Even in a savage tribe, the achievements of adults are far beyond what the immature members would be capable of if left to themselves. With the growth of civilization, the gap between the original capacities of the immature and the standards and customs of the elders increases. Mere physical growing up, mere mastery of the bare necessities of subsistence will not suffice to reproduce the life of the group. Deliberate effort and the taking of thoughtful pains are required. Beings who are born not only unaware of, but quite indifferent to, the aims and habits of the social group have to be rendered cognizant of them and actively interested. Education, and education alone, spans the gap.

Society exists through a process of transmission quite as much as biological life. This transmission occurs by means of communication of habits of doing, thinking, and feeling from the older to the younger. Without this communication of ideals, hopes, expectations, standards, opinions, from those members of society who are passing out of the group life to those who are coming into it, social life could not survive. If the members who compose a society lived on continuously, they might educate the new-born members, but it would be a task directed by personal interest rather than social need. Now it is a work of necessity.

EDUCATION IN PRAGMATISM

Pragmatists, in general, have chosen to focus on applied matters of education over more abstract or theoretical matters. Having a practical and hands-on education is highly valued by pragmatists as it will allow students to learn how to function in the world rather than to merely think about the world from a distance. The divisions between school and the real world ought to be erased. A good education is achieved by having one foot in school and one foot in the world, metaphorically speaking. If we conceive of school as a precursor to real life, it will be far less effective and relevant. The idea that one goes to school in order to gain knowledge for its own sake is troubling to pragmatists. Students must learn about the world while learning how to function within it—simultaneously knowing and doing.

The term education is a broader category for Dewey; schooling represents a subcategory of education. Schools (or schooling) are an important method for cultivating the immature. This method, however, is somewhat trivial as there are broader social institutions that play more significant roles in society.

Truth for the Individual and for Society

Dewey's views may be described as naturalistic, in keeping with most other pragmatist doctrines, and he claims we should seek knowledge as a tool for action and for managing our activities in a world filled with unknown challenges and problems. If we act on our knowledge and it allows us to solve problems and function in the world, then we may say that such knowledge is true. Ideas are instruments and Dewey's perspective is often referred to as instrumentalism.

Dewey argues that too many philosophers have made contemplation the highest goal. Too often, this kind of knowing or thinking fails to realize the importance of action. Many, perhaps most, traditional philosophers have been disconnected from life and are simply outdated and irrelevant. Dewey points out that many once-important questions have been forgotten and left unsolved because they lost vitality. However, many dead questions remain rooted in tradition, despite the lack of relevance. Dewey believes that the chief task of philosophers today is to remove the obstacles of previous thought that stand in the way of progress. When we learn to see contemporary questions in terms of the practical demands they place on our lives in the present rather than the abstract philosophical puzzles they pose from the past, Dewey believes that we will be better able to progress as a society.

Added to the problem of achieving contemporary relevance is that cultures are constantly undergoing change. Values and beliefs are changing; Dewey argues that the swiftness of change is something most of us are unprepared to deal with or adapt to. As a result, we are faced with a contradiction: we are living in the present, but our theories and beliefs often reflect the past. Education and philosophy should offer ways of overcoming the contradiction. We need new ways of thinking and acting, ways that are relevant to our social environments.

It is important to note that while Dewey views truth as what works in our individual lives, it is also what works for society. Early pragmatists emphasized the idea that truth is what works for individuals, but this created difficulties because it included those with corrupt or evil desires. Later pragmatists emphasize the idea of truth that is socially relevant. The truth of one society at a given time will be different than another's, but for both, their particular truth is what allows them to function.

Democracy

In his *Democracy and Education,* Dewey argues that democracy is more than merely a political form of thinking. It is an important process through which students develop and grow. Democracy describes a way of living, rather than an abstract political theory or ideal. Democracy is so intertwined with life experience that it allows us to see the world in ways that are unavailable to those not living within democratic societies.

The foundation of education is experience and, for Dewey, healthy experiences have a scientific (empirical and experimental) and democratic nature. When we appreciate the nature of experience, it becomes obvious how we ought to structure our educational environments. Education is the fundamental method by which social progress is achieved; done democratically, it allows us to formulate our world in progressive ways. A free society will not happen by accident—we must educate ourselves, thereby establishing freedom based on democratic principles.

Societies (re)create themselves and cultures are (re)formed through educational beliefs and activities. It is no surprise then that Dewey sees a very close connection between the development of a strong democratic nation and a sound philosophy of education. However, there are no hard and fast rules by which to implement education. Instead, it will always be an open-ended and perpetual activity of adapting, evaluating, and testing ideas and actions. To achieve moral equality, an important theme for Dewey, we need a democratic society willing to challenge tradition through experimentation and active participation. Each of us should be able to realize our own interests and goals without fear of being marginalized. We should be free to act in the most relevant and meaningful manner we think necessary. Each of us, when given the opportunity, may offer something unique to our communities, but only if we are given the freedom to engage and learn through our own interests.

CONSIDER:

Should the values of a society be illustrated in its educational system?

What should a progressive education look like?

What would a successful program of education look like? How can we judge success?

Do you see merit in the pragmatist approach?

Biology and Society

Influenced by Darwin's evolutionary theory, Dewey considers the science of biology an important aspect to his philosophy of education. We evolve as a species rather than individuals and individuals represent their collective experience of society. Our individuality is a repository for our societies. Dewey believes that it is through each of us that the group exists and there is an incontrovertible connection between individuality and community, and therefore the evolution of our species.

Education initiates us "into the interests, purposes, information, skill, and practices of mature members: Otherwise the group will cease its characteristic life" (*Democracy and Education*). Education of the individual reflects Dewey's interest in the larger group. If we can educate the young to understand the common end of society, so that they become interested and engaged participants, then we will have succeeded in fostering the development of individuals in a democratic body.

Education is often understood to be the acquisition of skills needed to perform future job tasks and social responsibilities. Dewey recognized that evolution rewards those who are open and adaptable. If we approach education as simply learning a list of specific skills, we will be discouraging the most adaptable kind of persons. One of the lessons Dewey takes from biology is that education must create people capable of learning more than simply those things or ideas set before them. Education must engage students in life from the very beginning in an active and interested manner. It must encourage creative and adaptive creatures able to flourish in unpredictable environments.

The primary goal of education is growth. Growth should lead to more growth, through which we learn, from our ongoing experiences, not only how to survive but how to flourish. Experience begets more experience, more learning, *ad infinitum*. When we fail to learn, we are effectively stopping ourselves from having healthy life experiences. To grow through education is to develop new habits capable of helping us live effectively. The danger, of course, is that we develop unthinking habits detached from reason. Instead, we must be cautious of unthinking habits. Education is a process of continually rethinking, recreating, and growing.

Traditional and Progressive Education

Dewey's philosophy is a response to the perceived failures of both traditional and so-called progressive theories of education. The traditional view of education, and most common, is often described as curriculum-centred. We might imagine this model in terms of the stereotypical scene in which students sit at desks, listening to lectures, with the expectation of learning information from books and the fixed knowledge preselected by those who have little or no knowledge of the

Foundations of Education

particular life situations of students. The overarching idea of progress is the expectation of learning specific things at specific times in order to move toward becoming a knowledgeable and functional citizen. In the traditional model, students are prepared for life after school. It is not uncommon today to have standardized tests meant to judge whether or not students have been adequately prepared in accordance with predetermined ends, specific criteria set out in advance, regardless of student interests, aptitudes, and individual needs.

The traditional model is often criticized for an overreliance on authority and structure. It is too formulaic. The routine and rigid format of education is said to steamroll the individuality of students. Governments and education boards may, in actuality, be driving students away from learning opportunities because many students will not fit approved curriculum plans. In contrast to the traditional model, progressive education is often described as student-centred. While progressivists may agree with traditionalists that subject matter is important, they disagree that it should take priority over the natural inclinations of children. Like Rousseau, progressive theorists believe that we should allow students the freedom to explore life spontaneously without inhibitive curriculum plans.

The progressive view is often criticized for its potential to create chaotic and unstructured learning environments. If we ignore the immaturity of students, critics warn, we are failing them. According to Dewey, we must find a way to harness their spontaneity and curiosity without stifling it, and simultaneously guide them by continually restructuring their educational contexts and challenging them in new ways.

Dewey recognizes that when children enter the classroom, they are already actively involved in the world. They have interests and goals from their home lives that need to be directed. The school environment should be a micro-society in which children are given opportunities to interact with real problems in a somewhat controlled setting. According to Dewey, the traditional view of education fails to sufficiently connect the interests of children to relevant subject matter. The formalization of learning tends to disconnect knowledge from action, and it is in this way that school fails to make sense to many students. We cannot simply write knowledge into them as if they are sponges or blank slates. Children must learn for themselves, which they will do when properly motivated, having realized the connection between theory and practice, or perhaps more accurately, having realized the relevance of theory to practice. If we force narrowly conceived notions of schooling onto the young we may end up limiting their perceptions of real life by creating a gap between formal education and the practical affairs of life.

While Dewey has been called a progressive theorist by some scholars, he is actually very critical of the progressivist failure to appropriately guide children. While we should give children the freedom to discover truth for themselves, we should not treat the interests of children as ends in themselves—both progressivists and traditionalists are too extreme.

CONSIDER:

What are the harms of formalized learning? Should we be concerned about boring students or alienating them from the subject matter of the world we want them to understand?
Should we encourage the spontaneity of children?
What do you think the merits and drawbacks are of allowing children to freely pursue their avenues of interest?

DEWEY'S LABORATORY SCHOOL

The Laboratory School was established in 1896 at the University of Chicago. Also called the "Dewey School," it was designed to show how a unity of knowledge and action could be achieved in education. Thinking and doing are inseparable; we should avoid thinking of theory and practice as two separate entities. The best kind of action is done in groups, communally, and integrates beliefs and ideas with action. The best curriculum concentrates on application, while avoiding radical abstractions. Science, math, arts, and social studies are to be taught through this kind of unity of knowledge and application.

116

An important part of Dewey's school was the establishment of explicit expectations between what a student did at the school and some kind of work that would be done by the student in his or her normal life. For instance, four- and five-year-olds might work on cooking or carpentry, while six-year-olds might plant wheat and cotton. These might seem like vocational skills, but such activities are also opportunities for students to develop basic scientific and social skills. Through experiencing real-life situations, students are able to see how problems develop, ask questions about how to solve problems, collaborate with others toward solving problems, apply different techniques, and test their ideas on given situations.

Dewey divided students into 11 different age groups. Depending on the age of the student, he or she might learn about historical events and ideas, scientific experiments, music, art, or languages, to name only a handful. Whatever the subject matter or skill, the student learns what is useful for solving problems related to their lives in meaningful ways. Again, the purpose of education is not to prepare students for life after school, but to engage them in life exercises at school.

Dewey saw his experimental school as an important vehicle for democracy. While building clubhouses or planting crops, children learn how to socialize democratically. Teachers did not motivate through fear of punishment but allowed children to organize themselves freely. The Laboratory School might be said to be democratic as well, as teachers had to continually adjust to the unique needs and requirements of the situation. A standard or fixed curriculum did not exist. Everyone in the school had to maintain an open and co-operative spirit of conversation. Moreover, everyone was in the same situation of continually experimenting to discover what works. Theories and actions had to be tested, critically judged, and adjusted.

The Role of the Teacher

Dewey realized that most teachers are poorly equipped for his school's unique form of teaching, which requires a great deal of knowledge and skill to be a facilitator rather than a dictator or centralized authority figure. This means that <u>teachers must be able to see the world from the perspective of students.</u>

For Dewey, the <u>job of every teacher</u> is to foster a good <u>disposition in the student, one who is adaptive, open, and critical.</u> The ideal student is one capable of self-realization. This student does not need to be told what to do and when to do it; rather, this <u>student will live with a certain sense of autonomy and responsibility.</u> However, this autonomy is not entirely self-interested. On the contrary, Dewey's ideal learner is one who is highly invested in the welfare of the larger community. Teachers cannot force students to live or think in specific ways, only help to maintain a learning environment that is congruent to democratic ideals.

Ultimately, the goal of the teacher—as with education more generally—is to help the student gain the dispositions and skills necessary for further education. Learning is rarely a terminal activity; rather, it is an ongoing process that fosters growth. We must continually improve and grow. As in Darwin's evolutionary biology, our success is not defined by specific achievements with definite ends, but by whether we are able to continue on in life being successfully adaptive and continually solving problems.

DEWEY'S PHILOSOPHY OF EDUCATION

Like Plato, Dewey ties education, knowledge, morality, and society together—the role of education being crucial to a healthy and strong society. Rousseau, by contrast, is highly dubious of any social education, for it will invariably lead to corrupting the natural inclinations of students. Dewey, Rousseau, and Locke differ regarding the importance of a formal schooling environment.

Dewey and Rousseau agree that students should be allowed to experience real problems rather than pretend or artificial problems. The ability to solve pretend problems does little to help students take genuine responsibility for real-world challenges. If students are to progress, they must be able and willing to connect their own actions with the world, and to do so without being forced by the teacher.

Another big difference is that Dewey does not think of a hierarchy of reason over passions, like Plato and Aristotle, but considers truth to be something we experience in our daily actions. Plato and Aristotle view truth as something lofty and abstract. Dewey's pragmatism may be said to tame a great deal of traditional philosophical thinking.

CR

DISCUSSION QUESTIONS AND LEARNING ACTIVITIES

1. What do you identify as the most significant implications of Dewey's philosophy for contemporary schooling systems, specifically public schools?
2. Design a curriculum for your own experimental school.
   a) What ideals would you have as guides for your school?
   b) How would you implement such a school in your own community?
3. Do you agree that there is a strong connection between democracy and education?
4. How far should a student be lead by a teacher? How much influence or control should a teacher have over a student's learning environment?
5. Have you ever been in a situation where you were not allowed to explore an idea or problem because of a traditional schooling system or expectation?
6. Should we force students to learn something they are not interested in learning?

Glossary

Aesthetics: Aesthetics focuses on the value pertaining to art and beauty.

Analytic Philosophy: The analytic approach to philosophy is characterized primarily by its emphasis on the rational analysis of language.

Auxiliaries: Auxiliaries (or guards) are, in Plato's system, those who enforce the will of the philosopher kings.

Creativity: To create means to fashion or produce something new.

Determinism: Determinism states, generally, that we are biological creatures determined by our environments and physical nature.

Emotion: Emotions are our experiences of various feelings, including intuition, fear, happiness, and so on.

Enlightenment: Beginning in late 17th- and 18th-century Europe, the Enlightenment shifted social and intellectual foundations away from tradition, religion, and superstition, toward reason, scientific method, and humanism.

Epistemology: Epistemology is the branch of thought that deals with principles of knowledge and human knowing.

Ethics: Ethics is the branch of philosophy that deals with questions concerning the rightness or wrongness of actions.

Existential Philosophy: The existential approach is characterized by its distain for abstractions, rules of logic and argumentation, and obsession with objectivity. A proper philosophical analysis must focus on the human being in his or her practical encounters with others and the world.

External World Skepticism: Even if we accept that knowledge is probably true, we still cannot really know much, if anything, about the world beyond our own immediate experiences.

Freewill: Freewill refers to the notion that humans are capable of making decisions free from interferences such as coercion and prejudice.

Golden Mean: According to Aristotle, in our daily activities we ought to strive toward a middle ground, a mean between extremes. Our actions and character ought to reflect a gold mean.

Guards: Guards (or auxiliaries) are, in Plato's system, those who enforce the will of the philosopher kings.

Hedonism: Hedonism is the view that the primary good in life is maximizing pleasure and minimizing pain.

Idealism: Idealism argues that reality is in some way a production of the mind.

Inductive Skepticism: If one of our primary means of knowing is to look for patterns in experience, we need to be relatively confident that the past will resemble the future.

Intellectual Virtue: Intellectual virtue, for Aristotle, refers to the excellence of our reason.

Logic: Logic is the branch of philosophy that deals with principles of reasoning and is used as a tool to clarify thought.

Masses: The masses, in Plato's system, are made up of everyone in society with the exception of philosopher kings and auxiliaries (or guards).

Metaphysics: Metaphysics is the study of ultimate reality.

Modern: Modernists believe reason is capable of saving humanity from its many vices.

Moral Virtue: Moral virtue, for Aristotle, refers to excellence of character, and it is connected to the desiring or passionate part of our souls.

Natural Man: Rousseau invites us to envision the primitive human being living without laws or society as basically good. By imagining "the natural man," Rousseau wants us to consider how society corrupts the self that is naturally non-social.

Negative Education: Negative education, for Rousseau, is child-centred and is meant to foster autonomous thinking. Negative does not mean pessimistic; rather, it represents the child's freedom from constraint and conformity.

Ontology: Ontology is the study of being and existence. What is being and existence? Are there different forms of being and existence?

Phenomenological Philosophy: The phenomenological approach is characterized by a focus on what is given or what appears in our consciousness of things. Phenomenology is interested in what is seen or directly experienced.

Philosophy: The term philosophy comes from two words: *philos* and *sophy*. *Philos* is from the Greek for love or lover. *Sophia* is the Greek for wisdom. To be a philosopher is to be a lover of wisdom, to be in pursuit of wisdom.

Philosopher Kings: Philosopher kings are Plato's ideal leaders. They have been tested throughout their lives to see whether their judgment is affected by the hardships they face or if they are capable of keeping on the right path despite various temptations and difficulties.

Platonism: Platonism refers to the philosophy of Plato and subsequent philosophies that resemble his philosophy.

Polity: A polity is a recognizable society or government.

Postmodern: Postmodernists see the use of reason as a dangerous vice.

Pragmatism: Pragmatism refers to a particular doctrine of meaning. The basic doctrine is that the meaning of an idea or term has its meaning insomuch as it guides our conduct. Truth, generally speaking, has a necessary connection with workability or applicability. If a theory or idea works when applied, it may be said to be true.

Reason: Reason has numerous definitions. As a philosophical ideal, reason represents critical thinking that forms the basis of reliable understanding—rationality. Irrational thinking, by contrast, is widely considered less reliable, even dangerous.

Romanticism: Romanticism, beginning late 18th-century Europe, challenged the ideal of reason by arguing that we ought to give emphasis to emotion instead.

Solipsism: Solipsism refers to the idea that the only thing that exists for sure is one's own mind.

Speculative Philosophy: The speculative approach to philosophy is characterized by a big-picture mentality. Speculative philosophy represents the most popular image of traditional philosophy.

Value Theory: Value theory covers a range of approaches to understanding how, why, and to what degree people value things—whether the thing valued is a person, idea, or object.